✦

Alone in the Kitchen
with an Eggplant

✦

◆

EDITED BY

Jenni Ferrari-Adler

RIVERHEAD BOOKS

a member of Penguin Group (USA) Inc.

NEW YORK

2007

◆

Alone
✦ IN THE ✦
Kitchen
✦ WITH AN ✦
Eggplant

✦

CONFESSIONS OF COOKING
FOR ONE
AND DINING ALONE

✦

RIVERHEAD BOOKS
Published by the Penguin Group
Penguin Group (USA) Inc., 375 Hudson Street, New York, New York 10014, USA ·
Penguin Group (Canada), 90 Eglinton Avenue East, Suite 700, Toronto, Ontario M4P 2Y3,
Canada (a division of Pearson Penguin Canada Inc.) · Penguin Books Ltd, 80 Strand,
London WC2R 0RL, England · Penguin Ireland, 25 St Stephen's Green, Dublin 2, Ireland
(a division of Penguin Books Ltd) · Penguin Group (Australia), 250 Camberwell Road,
Camberwell, Victoria 3124, Australia (a division of Pearson Australia Group Pty Ltd) ·
Penguin Books India Pvt Ltd, 11 Community Centre, Panchsheel Park, New Delhi–110 017,
India · Penguin Group (NZ), 67 Apollo Drive, Rosedale, North Shore 0745, Auckland,
New Zealand (a division of Pearson New Zealand Ltd) · Penguin Books (South Africa)
(Pty) Ltd, 24 Sturdee Avenue, Rosebank, Johannesburg 2196, South Africa

Penguin Books Ltd, Registered Offices: 80 Strand,
London WC2R 0RL, England

Library of Congress Cataloging-in-Publication Data

Ferrari-Adler, Jenni.
Alone in the kitchen with an eggplant : confessions of cooking for one and dining alone /
edited by Jenni Ferrari-Adler.
p.   cm.
ISBN 978-1-59448-947-1
1. Cookery for one.   I. Ferrari-Adler, Jenni.   II. Title.
TX652.F467   2007   2007001593
641.5'61—dc22

Printed in the United States of America
1 3 5 7 9 10 8 6 4 2

Book design by Marysarah Quinn

The recipes contained in this book are to be followed exactly as written. The publisher is not
responsible for your specific health or allergy needs that may require medical supervision. The
publisher is not responsible for any adverse reactions to the recipes contained in this book.

While the author has made every effort to provide accurate telephone numbers and Internet
addresses at the time of publication, neither the publisher nor the author assumes any responsibility for errors, or for changes that occur after publication. Further, the publisher does not
have any control over and does not assume any responsibility for author or third-party web-
sites or their content.

For Jofie

Contents

◆

It is the privilege of loneliness; in privacy one may do as one chooses.

—VIRGINIA WOOLF,

Mrs. Dalloway

Dinner alone is one of life's pleasures. Certainly cooking for oneself reveals man at his weirdest. People lie when you ask them what they eat when they are alone. A salad, they tell you. But when you persist, they confess to peanut butter and bacon sandwiches deep fried and eaten with hot sauce, or spaghetti with butter and grape jam.

—LAURIE COLWIN,

"Alone in the Kitchen with an Eggplant,"

Home Cooking

◆

◆

Alone in the Kitchen
with an Eggplant

◆

Introduction

Call it seven-thirty on a Wednesday night. No one else is home. A slight hunger hums in your body, so you wander into the kitchen. In front of the window a plant's stems wave like arms from their hanging basket. In the pantry bin, potatoes eye the onions slipping out of their skins. An apron hangs from the closet door like the shadow of a companion. Reflexively, you open the refrigerator and nod at the condiments, grab the hot sauce, and close the others back into cold darkness. Bottle of sauce in hand, you gaze around the room, inspecting the contents of the cabinets, the pile of paper menus from nearby restaurants, the spines of your cookbooks. You turn from the bookshelf and catch a glimpse of yourself in the window. In the heat, your hair has puffed wildly. You experience one of those weird lost minutes inside your head. Loneliness, you think, *loneliness* with its lyrical sound; you look like a lone lioness. You hear Alvy Singer, the young Woody Allen character from *Annie Hall*, say, "The universe is expanding." Bananas Shaughnessy from *The House of Blue Leaves* cuts him off: "My troubles all began a year ago—two years ago today— Two days ago today? Today." Then you remember your mother mixing cream cheese and lox into a pan of scrambling eggs.

You don't need a literal eggplant on hand to realize—with the pleasurable shock that comes from recognizing a small truth—that you are alone in the kitchen with one.

This book had its genesis in August 2004, when I spent the first of many such nights alone in Michigan. I was twenty-seven, a born-and-raised New Yorker, and I'd never lived by myself before. It was unsettling to be without a job or roommates, to have so much time alone in my tiny house in Ann Arbor. As a graduate student in fiction writing, I spent a few hours each day at my desk, following my characters around and trying to get them into interesting trouble. That left a lot of downtime. I ran on the treadmill at the YMCA, hiked in the arboretum, and drank many solitary cups of coffee. I hauled my laptop and bag from one café to another until it started to seem as if the hauling itself were my job. I was seeking, I suppose, some form of company and conversation, even if the majority of conversations were ones I merely overheard.

In my first semester I took a literature course, Exile and Homecoming, that contributed to my somewhat indulgent delusion that I was in exile. Where was the subway? Where were the bodegas and stoops? Where was my mother? Through the windows of my house I watched the neighbors rake leaves in the autumn and shovel snow in the winter. On the floor of my kitchen was a hopeful dog bowl—I didn't have a dog—and on the refrigerator were photographs of a boyfriend, a family, and friends. I had a life but I seemed to have abandoned it. Some days it required an act of will to believe my life still existed or mattered.

"Why does living alone feel so familiar?" I asked my little brother one night on the phone. He was living in a studio apartment in Philadelphia.

"Because it's like *being* alone," he said.

He was right, of course. Being alone—battling loneliness—was something at which I had always felt it was important to improve. Taking solitude in stride was a sign of strength and of a willingness to take care of myself. This meant—among other things—working productively, remembering to leave the house, and eating well. I thought about food all the time. I had subscriptions to *Gourmet* and *Food & Wine*. Cooking for others had often been my way of offering care. So why, when I was alone, did I find myself trying to subsist on cereal and water? I'd need to learn to cook for one.

It wasn't my first time in the Midwest. I'd done my undergraduate work—as I was learning to call it—at Oberlin College, which boasts many strange and wonderful things, one of which is a system of eating cooperatives. Students can opt out of the dining hall and into one of the communal dining rooms—if a room that seats eighty with folding chairs at round tables and is swept three times a day but is always dirty can be called a dining room. The kitchen featured four industrial-size mixers, two walk-in coolers, and a wok so enormous it doubled as a sled in winter. On the kitchen prep team, I diced eighty onions, wearing sunglasses that didn't stop my tears. When none of the vegetables I ordered came in on time, I still had to produce a stir-fry. I stood on a stool and begged brown rice not to burn. In some ways, learning to cook at Oberlin resembled learning to cook in a restaurant, only it was less precise. The diners charged the food the moment we set the big pots down.

After college, I followed the graduated masses to Brooklyn. I moved into a railroad apartment with two friends who had also gone through Oberlin's cooperative system. It seemed natural to us to make dinner together every night, and I gradually learned to cook for smaller groups. One of my roommates worked at the farmers' market and always brought home bags of vegetables. I worked, briefly, at a bakery in the neighborhood. At the end of the day I brought home bread; I had literally become the bread-winner of our makeshift household. Often, we had guests to dinner. We carried the food from the kitchen down the long hallway to the living room. We sat on the floor.

Over the next five years, we moved from neighborhood to neighborhood in Brooklyn. First, my boyfriend moved in with my friends and me. Later, he and I moved into our own place. Cooking for two was hard. I always made too much.

Now, marooned in the Midwest once again, I tried to live on a stipend. I tried to remember how to make friends. After class, I asked two girls if they wanted to go to a movie over the weekend and the asking made me blush. I tried to string together late-night telephone calls and infrequent visits into an approximation of a relationship. I missed eating salad and cheese with my boyfriend and going over the stories of our days. I missed the texture and chaos of daily life shared with others.

But if time were money, I was rich. There were hours, at least in the beginning, everywhere I looked. In addition to time, I had a galley kitchen, a shelf of cookbooks, two heavy pots, and a chef's knife. I lived near the farmers' market, a cooperative grocery, and a butcher shop. My bicycle had a basket. Which is all to say it was an excellent domestic setup.

But not only did I like to cook *for* others, I liked to cook *with* others. Would cooking alone be depressing? More or less depressing than living on sandwiches? More or less depressing than takeout?

"A potato," I told my brother, when he asked what I'd eaten for dinner. "Boiled, cubed, sautéed with olive oil, sea salt, and balsamic vinegar."

"That's it?" he asked. He was one to talk. He'd enjoyed what he called "bachelor's taco night" for three dinners and counting.

"A red cabbage, steamed, with hot sauce and soy sauce," I said the following night.

"Do you need some money?" he asked.

But it wasn't that, or it wasn't only that. I liked to think of myself not as a student on a budget, but rather as a peasant, a member of a group whose eating habits, across cultures, had long appealed to me.

"Are you full?" my brother asked.

"Full enough," I said.

"What about protein?"

Later that week, I diced two onions and sautéed them until they turned translucent and transformed the kitchen with their comforting smell. Flanked by books and magazines, I ate straight out of the pot at the table, my knees curled up to my chest. Aimee Mann sang from the stereo: *One is the loneliest number.*

Everything, I realized, growing light-headed, *anything* was delicious. In the next weeks I continued on in phases, first everything raw, then everything baked. I prioritized condiments. What wasn't delicious with Sriracha Hot Chili Sauce?

One night, I invited a few people from my program to dinner. For them, I made a salad with romaine lettuce, radishes, string beans, scallions, homemade croutons, and goat cheese. For them, I served dessert—pistachio nuts and chocolate chips in ramekins, a combination discovered via random out-of-cabinet consumption. At my nudging, surely, the conversation turned to the topic of cooking for ourselves. One woman's solitary dish was spaghetti carbonara. It satisfied her cravings for bacon, eggs, and pasta, and it made good leftovers. One man mixed couscous with canned soup. We agreed that dividing recipes by four was depressing, and that in cooking for ourselves, presentation went out the window.

When I considered it later, though, I had to admit I liked my personal presentation: the red pot with the flat wooden serving spoon, a half sheet of paper towel for a napkin. I liked my mismatched thrift-store plates, chopsticks, and canning jars. I even liked, I'm sorry to say, eating sandwiches while walking to class.

There was real pleasure to be had eating ice cream out of the container and pickles out of a glass jar, standing up at the counter. I wondered whether the cravings associated with pregnancy were really only a matter of women feeling empowered to admit their odd longings to their husbands, to ask another person to bring them the eccentric combinations they'd long enjoyed in private. If I'd been able to completely forget about nutrition, I might have created a diet based only on pickles and ice cream, salty and sweet.

Alas, I was somewhat conscious of the link between what I ate and my health, and so the next night—having eaten all the ice cream and pickles in the house—I mixed black beans and brown rice. I couldn't help smiling to myself when I thought of the man from my dinner party fluffing couscous alone in his kitchen across town. Sharing stories of eating alone had made me less lonely.

After a stressful deadline in February—that bleak month when Ann Arbor hibernates and people hurry, hunched over in ski jackets, through the dark—I decided to reward myself with a good meal. I made Amanda Hesser's Airplane Salad: Bibb lettuce, white beans, smoked trout, and a sherry vinaigrette. While I ate, I read her essay "Single Cuisine."

"I know many women who have a set of home-alone foods," writes Hesser. "My friend Aleksandra, for instance, leans toward foods that are white in color."

My pulse quickened as though Hesser were whispering in my ear. This was all I really wanted—to be let in on other people's secrets. What better place to start than in their kitchens?

Remembering Laurie Colwin's essay "Alone in the Kitchen with an Eggplant," I quickly went to my living room and plucked the friendly *Home Cooking* from my bookshelf. I sat with the yellow paperback on my black couch. I giggled at the description of Colwin's absurdly small Greenwich Village apartment, "the coziest place on earth," where she did dishes in the bathtub. She'd brought her kitchen into my living room. My breathing deepened with gratitude. The connectedness I felt was the opposite of the drifting into space I'd experienced whenever I spent more than three consecutive nights alone. We read to feel close to people we don't know, to get into other people's heads. I get the same sensation of intimacy from following a recipe. I began to scheme: Hesser, Colwin, and me . . . maybe I could break the silence and help men and women everywhere be less alone together.

Because cooks love the social aspect of food, cooking for one is intrinsically interesting. A good meal is like a present, and it can feel goofy, at best, to give yourself a present. On the other hand, there is something life affirming in taking the trouble to feed yourself well, or even decently. Cooking for yourself allows you to be strange or decadent or both. The chances of liking what you make are high, but if it winds up being disgusting, you can always throw it away and order a pizza; no one else will ever know. In the end, the experimentation, the impulsiveness, and the invention that such conditions allow for will probably make you a better cook.

As the days lengthened and warmed and the town revealed itself again, I peered tentatively into the windows of restaurants. I read the menus and contemplated going inside to tell the hostess, "Just me."

In her classic essay "A Is for Dining Alone," M. F. K. Fisher proclaims: "Enough of hit-or-miss suppers of tinned soup and boxed biscuits and an occasional egg just because I had failed once more to rate an invitation."

Don't we all think about the experience of dining alone in restaurants? Women tend to both romanticize and fear it. We have a shared image of an enigmatic woman pulling off a solitary dinner with style, perhaps in Europe. I think men have less trouble with it, though I'm not sure. It's certainly easier if you sit at the counter, or if the hour is off—three is a nice time for lunch by yourself; lunch is easier than dinner—or if other patrons are eating by themselves, or if you have a book with you, or better yet, two books.

My friend Rachel won't do it, not under any conditions. It's because, she says, her family moved around so frequently when she was growing up and she spent a lot of time worrying about sitting alone in the cafeteria.

With the exception of a recent barbecue chicken salad at T.G.I. Friday's in the Detroit Metro Airport, I tend to enjoy solitary dining. I like sitting at a sushi bar by myself, watching the chef work. Or at a counter, where I can have an omelet and a bottomless cup of coffee and stay a long time.

The more interaction with a waiter required, the more challenging it becomes for me to maintain my cool. In truth, it doesn't take much—one couple seated too close, an intrusive waiter—for the experience to spin me off into the murk of self-pity.

As mentioned, my boyfriend was anywhere but here. He was in New York, acquiring and editing books. He was always on the lookout for new projects. I told him I had a great idea, either for the imprint where he worked or for another imprint at his company that published cookbooks: an anthology of essays on cooking for one and dining alone that could function as a cookbook as well as a lifting-off point for readers to follow their instincts and create their own idiosyncratic meals.

I wanted someone to create this book so I could have a copy. I imagined it as a friendly presence in my kitchen for those nights when I cooked for myself. When my boyfriend suggested I put the book together, as a kind of summer job, I was surprised and resistant. It sounded like a lot of work. It sounded complicated. But eventually I was persuaded. Who could make the precise book I imagined better than me?

The more I thought about it, the more surprised I was that a book like this didn't already exist. A quick search on Amazon turned up some books on cooking for one, but they tended toward the pragmatic; their focus was logistical and dietary, and not on the rich experience of solitary cooking and eating. I noted with a mixture of amusement and trepidation that based on my search words—"cooking for one"—the website suggested I might be interested in books on the subject of *cookery for people with mental disabilities*. I didn't find a single book on the subject of dining alone. It started to seem as if we were talking about a phenomenon that hadn't yet been recognized as a phenomenon. It started to seem like anthropology. Or sociology. Or something that belonged on the Discovery Channel.

The boyfriend, on a weekend trip to Ann Arbor, drove me to the library, where we pored over indexes looking for the words *one, alone, solitary, single,* etc. I wrote a proposal and found an agent, and early in the summer the project sold.

I put together a wish list of food and fiction writers and invited them to participate in the project. I asked them: Do you have a secret meal you make (or used to make) for yourself? Do you have a set of rituals for dining alone (at home or in a restaurant), or rules?

To my surprise, they responded, often enthusiastically. Some seemed as if they'd been waiting a long time to be asked.

Rosa Jurjevics, daughter of the late Laurie Colwin, responded to my invitation almost immediately, writing, in part:

> I'm not much of a cook, I'm afraid to say, but I have a few funny meals that I do like to cobble together. They are mostly comprised of comfort food from my childhood growing up with my mother, strange foods we both loved due to our collective salt tooth.

All autumn essays floated into my computer's inbox. How good it was to know that Ann Patchett used to eat oatmeal in Provincetown, like a plow horse, like generations of Patchetts before her; that Beverly Lowry and Marcella Hazan eat anchovies; that Ben Karlin makes a sauce that changed the very course of his life! Some contributors react to their parents—Dan Chaon prepares a spicier, wilder chili than his mother used to cook; Anneli Rufus, free from her mother's rules against carbohydrates, revels in making plain, starchy meals (and, like Amanda Hesser's friend, she wants them white). There are fantasies: Phoebe Nobles transforms for a season into the Asparagus Superhero; Jeremy Jackson sings the song of the black bean; Holly Hughes, the mother of three young children, imagines what she would cook if she could cook only for herself. Colin Harrison, drawing on decades of solitary lunches, searches for his next regular restaurant. Laura Dave's tale of cooking not only ends in but directly causes romantic love.

On the flip side, Jonathan Ames poisons himself with expired eggs, then basks in the comfort provided by the kind and bosomy waitress at his local diner. Erin Ergenbright writes from the perspective of a waitress serving a finicky solo diner and provides a recipe from the restaurant. Courtney Eldridge, not yet willing to produce the dishes her ex-husband, a chef, taught her to make, offers her mother's salsa recipe. Jami Attenberg braves a hotel buffet at a resort before retreating to the safety of room service.

With repeated readings I was able to inhabit each essay. I walked to Ann Arbor's Kerrytown Market to buy the ingredients for Steve Almond's *quesaritos*. At Steve's suggestion, I asked the fishmonger for tiger-tail shrimp to make myself seem cool. I made Jeremy Jackson's black beans and rice and thought of Jeremy up to his arms in dried beans. I wrapped myself up in a kimono and ate Nora Ephron's mashed potatoes, a perfect predecessor to Laura Calder's Kippers Mash, comfort food for a queen. It's almost impossible to make Marcella Hazan's *tost* without thinking of how her husband calls her *mangia panini* (sandwich eater), or Paula Wolfert's *pa amb tomàquet* without conjuring up her day of pure Mediterranean bliss, or Ben Karlin's salsa rosa without thinking about hash and Italy. If you do as Laura Dave instructs and listen to "Atlantic City" and drink two glasses of wine while you make beef stroganoff, it will be hard not to be swept into Laura's Manhattan, in which all things lonely and difficult become romantic, glazed with youth and hope. This book abounds with recipes, tips, idiosyncratic truths passed kitchen to kitchen, mouth to mouth.

My friend Rachel—she of the cafeteria fear—works for a nonprofit that advocates for independent farms. She feels weird mentioning my book to her colleagues, since their organization believes in community dining. I think this concern is intriguing but ultimately beside the point. My book is by no means a *suggestion* to eat alone; even the most community minded among us must occasionally find ourselves hungry and alone in the house. There are various reasons for solitary dining, only some of them a result of loss in its numerous forms. We adjust to solitude and an increased responsibility for caring for ourselves as we grow older, as we leave home for the first time, as we move, as our circumstances change. We dine alone once or for a brief time or for a long time.

I'm interested in finding out what happens then. Do we hold to the same standards that apply to cooking for others? Usually not, it seems. I'm interested in why.

In "Making Soup in Buffalo," Beverly Lowry writes: "The fact was, I *wanted* the same thing again and again. And so I yielded, bought the goods, took them home, cooked, ate, accompanied usually by music, preferably a public radio station that played music I liked. And I am here to tell you, the pleasure never diminished. I was happy every time."

Every time I read those sentences, I take a big breath and let it out with a sigh. Good, I think. I'll make the same weird meal I've been making all week—half a loaf of seven-grain bread sliced and slathered with tahini and honey—again tonight. It's what I want. It's delicious and filling.

It is my hope that some nights in your kitchen you will reach for this book and be comforted and laugh out loud with recognition—and try another recipe. These are essays to be read and reread, to be stained with gravy and wine. I've tried to assemble the book so it reads fluidly from beginning to end. Arranging the pieces gave me the sensation of designing the seating chart for the most wonderful dinner party in the world. The book can also be read backward, and each essay stands alone. In that way it is like a cookbook, like cooking. Of course, this anthology is by no means exhaustive; it is merely an entryway.

If you choose to give this book to yourself, to keep it in your kitchen, my hope is that it will give you some company, some inspiration, and some recipes that require no division or subtraction. I hope it will remind you that *alone* and *lonely* are not synonymous; you will have yourself—and the food you love— for company.

In conclusion, let me just say that a scoop of vanilla ice cream with a handful of walnuts (or broken pretzels) and maple syrup, served in a coffee cup, makes a perfect dessert for one person cross-legged on a couch, or, if it's warm out, on a porch or a stoop.

As an alternative—if right now you're rolling your eyes and thinking, *not so much with the ice cream*—allow me to recommend Fage Total 0% Greek yogurt with one teaspoon of honey mixed in. The honey does something not only to the flavor but to the texture of the yogurt, making it sublimely creamy and sweet. I like to use the teaspoon to eat the dessert out of the container. While I eat, I daydream about the dinner parties I will throw in the shimmering future, when I will serve this yogurt-and-honey creation in champagne glasses and be applauded for my culinary brilliance.

But for now, eating this in bed by myself is not merely fine, it is sweet.

Alone in the Kitchen with an Eggplant
LAURIE COLWIN

For eight years I lived in a one-room apartment a little larger than the *Columbia Encyclopedia*. It is lucky I never met Wilt Chamberlain because if I had invited him in for coffee he would have been unable to spread his arms in my room, which was roughly seven by twenty.

I had enough space for a twin-sized bed, a very small night table, and a desk. This desk, which I use to this day, was meant for a child of, say, eleven. At the foot of my bed was a low table that would have been a coffee table in a normal apartment. In mine it served as a lamp stand, and beneath it was a basket containing my sheets and towels. Next to a small fireplace, which had an excellent draw, was a wicker armchair and an ungainly wicker footstool which often served as a table of sorts.

Instead of a kitchen, this minute apartment featured a metal counter. Underneath was a refrigerator the size of a child's playhouse. On top was what I called the stove but which was only two electric burners—in short, a hot plate.

Many people found this place charming, at least for five

minutes or so. Many thought I must be insane to live in so small a space, but I loved my apartment and found it the coziest place on earth. It was on a small street in Greenwich Village and looked out over a mews of shabby little houses, in the center courtyard of which was a catalpa tree. The ceiling was fairly high—a good thing since a low one would have made my apartment feel like the inside of a box of animal crackers.

My cupboard shelves were so narrow that I had to stand my dinner plates on end. Naturally, there being no kitchen, there was no kitchen sink. I did the dishes in a plastic pan in the bathtub and set the dish drainer over the toilet.

Of course there was no space for anything like a dining room table, something quite unnecessary as there was no dining room. When I was alone I ate at my desk, or on a tray in bed. When company came I opened a folding card table with a cigarette burn in its leatherette top. This object was stored in a slot between my countertop and my extremely small closet. Primitive as my kitchen arrangements were, I had company for dinner fairly often.

I moved in one cool summer day when I was twenty-three. That night I made dinner for two college friends who were known as the Alices since they were both named Alice and were best friends. I remember our meal in detail. A young man had given me a fondue pot as a moving-in present. These implements, whose real function was to sit unused on a top shelf collecting furry coats of dust, were commonly given as wedding and housewarming presents in the sixties and are still available at garage sales of the eighties. They were made of stainless steel and sat on a three-legged base at the bottom of which was a ring to hold a can of Sterno. Along with the pot came four long-handled forks, two of which I have to this day. (They are extremely useful for spearing string beans and for piercing things that have fallen onto the floor of your oven.) The fellow who gave it to me was fond of a place called Le Chalet Suisse, where I had once enjoyed beef fondue. I felt it would be nice to replicate this dish for my friends.

I served three sauces, two of which I made: one was tomato based and the other was a kind of vinaigrette. The third was béarnaise in a jar from the local delicatessen. I bought sirloin from the butcher and cubed it myself. When my two friends came, I lit the can of Sterno and we waited for the oil to heat.

While we waited we ate up all the bread and butter. One of the Alices began to eat the béarnaise sauce with a spoon. The other Alice suggested we go out for dinner. Once in a while we would dip a steak cube into the oil to see what happened. At first we pulled out oil-covered steak. After a while, the steak turned faintly gray. Finally, I turned one of my burners on high and put the pot on the burner to get it started. Thereafter we watched with interest as our steak cubes sizzled madly and turned into little lumps of rubbery coal. Finally, I sautéed the remaining steak in a frying pan. We dumped the sauces on top and gobbled everything up. Then we went to the local bar for hamburgers and French fries.

It took me a while to get the hang of two burners. Meanwhile, my mother gave me a toaster oven, thinking this would ensure me a proper breakfast. My breakfast, however, was bacon and egg on a buttered roll from an underground cafeteria at the Madison Avenue side of the Lexington Avenue stop of the E train. My toaster oven was put to far more interesting use.

I began with toasted cheese, that staple of starving people who live in garrets. Toasted cheese is still one of my favorite foods and I brought home all sorts of cheese to toast. Then, after six months of the same dinner, I turned to lamb chops. A number of fat fires transpired, none serious enough to call the fire department. I then noticed after a while that my toaster oven was beginning to emit a funny burnt rubber smell when I plugged it in. This, I felt, was not a good sign and so I put it out on the street. With the departure of my toaster oven, I was thrown back, so to speak, on my two burners.

Two-burner cooking is somewhat limiting, although I was constantly reading or being read to about amazing stove-top feats: people who rigged up gizmos on the order of a potato baker and baked bread in it, or a thing that suspended live coals over a pot so the tops of things could be browned, but I was not brave enough to try these innovations.

Instead, I learned how to make soup. I ate countless pots of lentil, white bean and black bean soup. I tried neck bones and ham hocks and veal marrow bones and bacon rinds. I made thousands of omelets and pans of my mother's special tomatoes and eggs. I made stewed chicken and vegetable stew. I made bowls of pickled cabbage—green cabbage, dark sesame oil, salt, ginger and lemon juice. If people came over in the afternoon, I made cucumber sandwiches with anchovy butter.

I would invite a friend or friends for Saturday night. Three people could fit comfortably in my house, but not four, although one famous evening I actually had a tiny dance party in my flat, much to the inconvenience of my downstairs neighbor, a fierce old Belgian who spent the afternoon in the courtyard garden entertaining his lady friends. At night he generally pounded on his ceiling with a broom handle to get me to turn my music down. My upstairs neighbor, on the other hand, was a Muncie, Indiana, Socialist with a limp. I was often madly in love with him, and sometimes he with me, but in between he returned my affections by stomping around his apartment on his gimpy leg—the result of a motorcycle accident—and playing the saxophone out the window.

On Saturday mornings I would walk to the Flavor Cup or Porto Rico Importing coffee store to get my coffee. Often it was freshly roasted and the beans were still warm. Coffee was my nectar and my ambrosia: I was very careful about it. I decanted my beans into glass and kept them in the fridge, and I ground them in little batches in my grinder.

I wandered down Bleecker Street, where there were still a couple of pushcarts left, to buy vegetables and salad greens. I went to the butcher, then bought the newspaper and a couple of magazines. Finally I went home, made a cup of coffee and stretched out on my bed (which, when made and pillowed, doubled as a couch), and I spent the rest of the morning in total indolence before cooking all afternoon.

One Saturday I decided to impress a youth whose mother, a Frenchwoman, had taught him how to cook. A recipe for pot roast with dill presented itself to me and I was not old or wise enough to realize that dill is not something you really want with your pot roast. An older and wiser cook would also have known that a rump steak needs to be baked in the oven for a long time and does not fare well on top of the stove. The result was a tough, gray wedge with the texture of a dense sponge. To pay me back and show off, this person invited me to his gloomy apartment, where we ate jellied veal and a strange pallid ring that quivered and glowed with a faintly purplish light. This, he told me, was a cold almond shape.

The greatest meal cooked on those two burners came after a night of monumental sickness. I had gone to a party and disgraced myself. The next morning I woke feeling worse than I had ever felt in my life. After two large glasses of seltzer and lime juice, two aspirins and a morning-long nap, I began to feel better. I spent the afternoon dozing and reading Elizabeth David's *Italian Food*. By early evening I was out of my mind with hunger but feeling too weak to do anything about it. Suddenly, the doorbell rang and there was my friend from work. She brought with her four veal scallops, a little bottle of French olive oil, a bunch of arugula, two pears and a Boursault cheese, and a loaf of bread from Zito's bakery on Bleecker Street. I would have wept tears of gratitude but I was too hungry.

We got out the card table and set it, and washed the arugula in the bathtub. Then we sautéed the veal with a little lemon, mixed the salad dressing and sat down to one of the most delicious meals I have ever had.

Then, having regained my faculties, I felt I ought to invite the couple at whose house I had behaved so badly. They were English. The husband had been my boss. Now they were going back to England and this was my chance to say good-bye.

At the time I had three party dishes: Chicken with sesame seeds and broccoli. Chicken in an orange-flavored cream sauce. Chicken with paprika and Brussels sprouts. But the wife, who was not my greatest fan, could not abide chicken and suggested, through her husband, that she would like pasta. Spaghetti alla Carbonara was intimated and I picked right up on it.

Spaghetti is a snap to cook, but it is a lot snappier if you have a kitchen. I of course did not. It is very simple to drain the spaghetti into a colander in your kitchen sink, dump it into a hot dish and sauce it at once. Since I had no kitchen sink, I had to put the colander in my bathtub; my bathroom sink was too small to accommodate it. At this time my bathroom was quite a drafty place, since a few weeks before a part of the ceiling over the bath had fallen into the tub, and now as I took my showers, I could gaze at exposed beams. Therefore the spaghetti, by the time the sauce hit it, had become somewhat gluey. The combination of clammy pasta and cream sauce was not a success. The look on the wife's face said clearly: "You mean you dragged me all the way downtown to sit in an apartment the size of a place mat for *this*?"

When I was alone, I lived on eggplant, the stove-top cook's strongest ally. I fried it and stewed it, and ate it crisp and sludgy, hot and cold. It was cheap and filling and was delicious in all manner of strange combinations. If any was left over I ate it cold the next day on bread.

Dinner alone is one of life's pleasures. Certainly cooking for oneself reveals man at his weirdest. People lie when you ask them what they eat when they are alone. A salad, they tell you. But when you persist, they confess to peanut butter and bacon sandwiches deep fried and eaten with hot sauce, or spaghetti with butter and grape jam.

I looked forward to nights alone. I would stop to buy my eggplant and some red peppers. At home I would fling off my coat, switch on the burner under my teakettle, slice up the eggplant, and make myself a cup of coffee. I could do all this without moving a step. When the eggplant was getting crisp, I turned down the fire and added garlic, tamari sauce, lemon juice and some shredded red peppers. While this stewed, I drank my coffee and watched the local news. Then I uncovered the eggplant, cooked it down and ate it at my desk out of an old Meissen dish, with my feet up on my wicker footrest as I watched the national news.

I ate eggplant constantly: with garlic and honey, eggplant with spaghetti, eggplant with fried onions and Chinese plum sauce.

Since many of my friends did not want to share these strange dishes with me, I figured out a dish for company. Fried eggplant rounds made into a kind of sandwich of pot cheese, chopped scallions, fermented black beans and muenster cheese. This, with a salad and a loaf of bread, made a meal. Dessert was *always* brought in. Afterwards I collected all the pots and pans and silverware and threw everything into my pan of soapy water in the bathtub and that was my dinner party.

Now I have a kitchen with a four-burner stove, and a real fridge. I have a pantry and a kitchen sink and a dining room table. But when my husband is at a business meeting and my little daughter is asleep, I often find myself alone in the kitchen with an eggplant, a clove of garlic and my old pot without the handle about to make a weird dish of eggplant to eat out of the Meissen soup plate at my desk.

Dinner for One, Please, James
ANN PATCHETT

In the winter of 1990 I was twenty-six years old, broke, and living alone in Provincetown, Massachusetts. Winter at the end of Cape Cod was a lonely proposition but since I have always been fond of being alone it was not at all a bad one. I had come to the Fine Arts Work Center as part of a fellowship program that gives ten artists and ten writers seven off-season months in which to work. We had a place to live and a stipend of $350 a month, which covered food, the phone bill, and anything else one can think of to buy when there's very little money and no place to spend it.

I got along fine. Being broke and isolated is usually associated with hardship but it's actually quite conducive to writing a novel. Like the scrubby little trees that grew in the sand near the ocean, I found I could thrive on neglect. Everything in the town that bustled and glimmered in the summer months had folded up its tent and left by the time I arrived in October. The fruit stands boarded over, the restaurants closed down. Only a stalwart bar or two hung on to keep the locals from going completely mad. The A&P on Shank Painter Road sold fewer goods during reduced hours for what seemed to me to be exorbitantly high prices. In short, The Season was over.

I had a very small apartment on the second floor of a house. One room was a kitchen and the other was a bedroom that was not much bigger than a twin mattress. I wrestled the bed into the kitchen so that I could call the bedroom a study, a study being the room I needed the most. As for sleeping in the kitchen, it made perfect sense to me. It was warmer in there, and in the morning I could get up and make my oatmeal and tea and take it straight back to bed.

Those seven months, long and cold and quiet, were really the first I'd ever spent completely by myself. At this tender age I had a great deal of experience being taken care of by other people, and a reasonable amount of experience taking care of someone else, but I'd never had the opportunity to see how I would fare when left completely to my own devices. When would I go to bed? Would I still be so neat? Would I drink too much or never drink at all? What would I make myself for supper?

The answer to this last one wasn't so impressive.

It turns out that where food was concerned, I had a seemingly endless capacity for repetition. Breakfast was a fixed tableau and boredom never even entered into it. As long as I was eating alone I ate oatmeal, as Patchetts have done for generations before me. Oatmeal was actually one of the more complicated things I made for myself because it required a heating element, though in truth I have eaten bowls of uncooked oats as well, pinching them up between my fingers and thumb and nibbling while I worked. They were as pleasing to me as they would have been to any plow horse. Lunch every day consisted of a tomato sandwich with mustard. I could get two lunches out of a single tomato, three if it was a whopper. Even in February, when tomatoes were orange and vaguely translucent with the texture of a softball, I was never deterred. If I was feeling very fancy for dinner I would scramble some eggs or pour jarred red sauce over pasta, but most nights did not feel fancy at all. I ate slices of white cheese on Saltines with a dollop of salsa, then smoothly transitioned to Saltines spread with butter and jam for dessert. I would eat as many as were required to no longer be hungry and then I would stop. All food that wasn't eaten sitting up in bed was eaten standing over the sink or sometimes in front of the refrigerator, where I looked around for things that weren't there. Day after day, week after month, I stuck to my routines like a chorus girl in the back row. I never minded. Even all these years later, in a life that is loaded with fancy supermarkets and disposable income, a Saltine is still delicious.

Perhaps this shameful dearth of culinary sophistication could all be explained away by my lack of options at the time: funds were low, the grocery store was barren, restaurants, if I could have afforded them, were closed. If this were only a matter of what I ate when times were tight, then it would be reduced to no more than a sad chapter in an otherwise bright gastronomic history. Except I wasn't sad, I was alone, and when I'm alone it's impossible for me to have any standards about eating.

This isn't because I don't know better. Even as I was putting the salsa on the cracker I knew about food. My mother, who could live entirely off of Kraft processed cheese singles and Shredded Wheat, can also make a perfect béchamel sauce. She taught my sister and me how to loosen the skin from a chicken and slip in fresh herbs, to fill the cavity with garlic and lemons. Time after countless time, I saw her poring over Julia Child in order to reinvent Thanksgiving or have a sit-down dinner for twelve or a cocktail party for a hundred. My sister and I were taught how to follow a recipe (it's only a matter of paying attention, like those eighth-grade reading comprehension tests) and when to leave the recipe behind and strike out on our own. In high school I excelled at home economics. I made crêpes and madeleines for French club. My first job in college was running the student bakery, getting up at five to bake a hundred cookies and several cakes before classes started. In the evenings I helped cook for dinner parties at the president's house. I made butter knots and osso buco. I whisked up salad dressing, simmered the flan. Being plain in my twenties, I seduced the boys I liked with shrimp creole and chocolate cake. I found my share of love. In graduate school I made special soft meals for my best friend, Lucy, who had lost half her jaw to cancer as a child and was limited by what she could chew. I worked as a line cook in a fancy vegetarian restaurant and burned my wrists and thumbs on the grill. I have a piecrust recipe that takes two days to make, and all of my pies, even the blueberry, serve up flawlessly from the first slice. I have been a waitress, a hostess, and briefly, at the age of twenty-four, a well-meaning wife who followed the classic food pyramid while putting dinner on the table every night.

The fact is, I love to feed other people. I love their pleasure, their comfort, their delight in being cared for. Cooking gives me the means to make other people feel better, which in a very simple equation makes me feel better. I believe that food can be a profound means of communication, allowing me to express my-self in a way that seems at times much deeper and more sincere than words. My Gruyère cheese puffs straight from the oven say *I'm glad you're here. Sit down, relax. I'll look after everything.*

So what does it say about my self-esteem that I know per-fectly well how to make a velouté and yet would choose to crack open a can of SpaghettiOs when dining alone? (I am not using the word "SpaghettiOs" as a metaphor here.) Do I not believe that I am entitled to the same level of tenderness that I extend to others? Or is it, in fact, a greater level of self-love to not put myself through the hassle of making dinner?

I think it is quite possible to be a very good cook while car-ing next to nothing about food. Just because you can prepare a dish doesn't mean you necessarily have any interest in eating it. I took far more pleasure in cooking for strangers in restaurants than I ever did having to sit down with my own guests. This is not a matter of having a preference for strangers, it's just that strangers tend not to want to eat with the help. Cooking is ex-hausting, and nothing kills my appetite like spending a day trim-ming the fat off of chicken or shredding a couple pounds of Brussels sprouts into paper-thin confetti without slicing off my fingertips. Sure, I can make a sole meunière, but it must be done over a flame that is fit to brighten up the very gates of hell. There is a split second in which to get it right, to get your side dishes on the plate, and get the plate to the table the very instant the fish is done while everything is still searing hot. I can do it, barely, but then can I eat it? My hair is slicked back with sweat, my hands tremble when I hold the fork, the smell of browned butter coats the inside of my nose. That is the moment I long to be in the shower, not at the table, and besides, it's impossible to both eat dinner and beat up a zabaglione.

So while it is a deep and genuine pleasure to nurture those I love, it is an equal pleasure to be off the hook for that responsibility as well, to pass over food that is delicate and beautiful and complex in flavor in favor of the item that is least likely to spoil. Eating as a simple means of ending hunger is one of the great liberties of being alone, like going to the movies by yourself in the afternoon or, back in those golden days of youth, having a cigarette in the bathtub. It is a pleasure to not have to take anyone else's tastes into account or explain why I like to drink my grapefruit juice out of the carton. Eating, after all, is a matter of taste, and taste cannot always be good taste. The very thought of maintaining high standards meal after meal is exhausting. It discounts all the peanut butter that is available in the world.

When I picked up my oldest friend, Tavia, for dinner last week we met at her father's apartment. Kent has lived alone for more than twenty years, since his girls grew up and moved out on their own. His home is small and overflowing with the artifacts of his life, the testaments of his pleasures and personal style. "Come to dinner with us," I said to him. Though I certainly would have enjoyed his company, I also was showing a certain amount of noblesse oblige: here he was, after all, alone. Why not be nice and bring him along?

"Oh, I couldn't," he said happily. "I've made lobster Newburg for dinner."

He had driven downtown to get the lobster tail at the fish stand in the farmers' market. It is no small trek. Alone, Kent did not wait around for any crumbs of company or lobster his daughters or their friends might have thrown him. Alone, Kent had seized his Wednesday night and gone ahead with his New-burg. That was his pleasure, unimaginable to me but neverthe-less deeply admired. I tried to picture myself turning down a similar invitation if I had a free evening. Could I stand my ground? Could I say no, in fact I've opened a fresh sleeve of Saltines tonight? Probably not. Probably I would lie. And then, after the visitors had left, I would stand over the sink and eat whatever was around, whatever I needed in order to go and do the work that I love. Even now it is a picture of heaven to me, an evening spent alone and well fed in the tradition of my own low standards, pure heaven.

Beans and Me

JEREMY JACKSON

Most beans are lowly, of course, but it seems to me that the pinto, the lentil, and the black bean are the lowliest of them all, and all the more charming because of it. Sometimes I picture these three beans holding hands and chiming together, "We're lowly! We're of the earth! We're beans for the people!" And sometimes, when I envision this trio, the black-eyed pea waddles into view and says, "Whaddabout me, guys?" And the pinto, the lentil, and the black bean say, "Hiya, black-eyed pea! Get in here! We didn't forget you!" Then they all sing some kind of bean song.

Lowliness, in my book, is a virtue, and therefore by telling you about my dream of the lowly beans I am simply revealing to you my favorite beans. And of all the beans I have loved in my lifetime—and there have been many—no bean stands above the black bean. The black bean reigns supreme. The black bean has the key to my heart. The black bean and me go way back.

Now, I should be clear here what I'm actually talking about. I'm not talking about dried black beans, glorious as they are. I mean, they're beautiful and cheap, and every time I see the big bin of them in the bulk aisle of my food co-op, I have to resist the urge to plunge my arms in up to my elbows. If I could, I would like to swim in a sea of dried black beans. But no, it's not dried black beans that I'm in love with. I'm in love with the canned ones. True, some people will say that using canned beans is cheating—like buying canned applesauce instead of making your own—and I understand that point of view. But to get dried black beans tender, in my experience, you have to boil them for approximately six days. You know what I say to that? Give me the can opener. Because inside that lovely little can o' beans are not only beans that are already cooked, but beans that are sitting in a bunch of their own gravy. Bingo! That's the good stuff.

I first met black beans in college. It was the early nineties, and things were looking up for black beans. In those days, I was flirting a lot with both vegetarianism and vegetarians, and black beans and rice was basically *the* standard meal that vegetarians on campus were making. My friend Sarah, who lived in a co-op dorm where the students did the cooking (just think of the amount of beans they went through there), showed me the very clever and unbeatable trick of stirring shredded cheese into the hot rice just before it was served with the beans. I still use this trick to this day, even though it does make a bit of a mess for whoever washes the rice pot. The mess is worth it, though.

By my senior year of college, I was cooking for myself, and black beans and rice was my favorite meal because it was fast, easy, cheap, and satisfying. I owned exactly one cookbook at that time, *The Moosewood Cookbook*, and it had a lot of credibility with me because it featured a knockout recipe called Brazilian Black Bean Soup.

I also relied on black beans throughout graduate school. I think that it was then that I started sometimes serving the beans with cornbread instead of rice—pouring the hot beans over the cornbread. This way of using cornbread was clearly something that was part of my Missouri heritage. It also, I realized, made for a fantastically complete dinner because cornbread, when topped with apple butter or just butter and honey, was a superb dessert.

Those were the early years of my black bean love. To be honest, a lot of the memories have faded somewhat, and many are gone completely. But all of the memories—the clear ones, the muddled ones, and the lost ones—are good. It was the courtship phase of my relationship with black beans. It was a golden time. It will dwell in my heart forever.

In the late nineties, at the alarming age of twenty-five, I returned to teach English at my alma mater. When I got the job, I was living in Missouri, and the logistics of looking for an apartment in upstate New York were awkward. Just when it seemed as if I would have to fly out there just to find an apartment, the office of faculty housing called me and told me that they had one opening. But it was a very small apartment, they explained, and it shared some kind of common entrance hallway with another apartment. Sounded fine to me, and the price—about two hundred a month—was so insanely low I had to take it. Plus, it was just across the street from campus.

My dad and I loaded his pickup truck and my car with my furniture and books and trekked east in late August. When we entered the new apartment, we liked the first room—a square little room that was about the size of a junior's dorm room—and we wondered what the second room would be like. We opened the door to the second room only to discover that it wasn't a second room. It was a closet. So the next day Dad headed home to Missouri with my sofa and a few other things still in the back of the pickup. They hadn't fit in the apartment.

That first semester of teaching, it quickly became clear that I didn't fit into the system. A few years ago, I'd been a student here, and happily so. But now I was too old and too square to socialize with the students. (Plus, it was kinda against the rules.) Likewise, I was too young and not boring enough to socialize with the professors. In addition, walking around campus was like walking through a landscape filled with ghosts, because though the place was the same—there was the window of my freshman room, there was my old girlfriend's apartment, there was the chair in the library I had fallen asleep in so many times—the people were different. All my friends were gone, excepting a couple of professors.

So, outside of the classroom I spent my time alone. I would scurry home before dark. My apartment was *cozy*, that's for sure. My mom had made curtains for the big bank of windows, and I would close the curtains, and turn on the radio to an AM station that played songs from fifty years earlier, and then I would start cooking dinner. I had no television. Cooking was my entertainment.

The other thing about the apartment was that it was bisected by a long entry hall that led to another apartment. On one side of the hall was my bedroom, with its own door, of course. On the other side of the hallway were my galley kitchen and bathroom. There was no door between the kitchen and hallway, and so whenever I was cooking dinner, I was standing just a few feet from the hallway, and invariably Mary Lou—a short librarian more than twice my age, with an unfortunate librarian haircut and a deeply held conviction that synthetic fabrics were evil— would come in, smell my dinner in progress, comment on how great it smelled, then shuffle into her apartment. She would then shuffle back out to walk her dog, shuffle back in a few minutes later, basically repeat how good my dinner smelled, and then disappear into her apartment for the evening. In other words, my cooking was a public affair. Many days, these interactions with Mary Lou about the aromas of my cooking were the only words anyone spoke to me all day.

What does a person cook for himself when dining alone every day? Lots of soup. Pasta. At least a few times a month I would make something new out of *The Moosewood Cookbook*, something nice. A treat. But truth be told, the best treat of all was a pot of hot black beans and fresh cornbread.

Maybe my *human* college friends weren't here anymore, but I'd also met black beans in college, and they were still with me. My friends, the beans. As for cornbread, well, cornbread and I went even farther back—to the edge of memory, to family meals, to my parents, my grandparents, my great-grandparents. So here, on my plate, I had a small assemblage of friends who knew me well. That was enough, for those two years I lived there. Beans and me and cornbread. That was just enough.

.   .   .

I remember once I was working late in my office, grading papers or maybe just playing Snood on the computer. It was in the autumn, I think, and I printed something out on the network and then went into the English Department office to retrieve the printout and there was my pal Dean, who'd been one of my professors just four years ago, but who was now my colleague. We chatted briefly and then he said why didn't we go and grab some dinner together?

It was a perfectly reasonable request. I liked Dean, and he had always been kind to me. (The summer between my junior and senior years of college he let me store several boxes of my belongings in his garage, for example.) But the problem was that I had retreated so far into myself—shielding myself from the ghosts and memories of this place—that I had become reliant upon the comfort of rituals and plans. I had already decided that I was going to have black beans and cornbread for dinner, and I had already picked out the can of beans—hours ago—and put it on my kitchen counter as a reminder. And I now found myself wanting, more than anything, to go home to enjoy my simple meal by myself. I stammered something about how I already had plans for dinner—even awkwardly mentioned the can of beans I had already picked out—and, bless him, Dean saw that he had hit upon a nerve and he told me that it was no problem at all and that we would have dinner another time. I agreed.

What does an introvert do when he's left alone? He stays alone.

. . .

At the end of my second year, I told the department I didn't want to teach a third year, and I started thinking of where I could move and be a writer full time. I got a house-sitting gig for the summer. It was a huge rambling farmhouse at the edge of campus, a full hundred and fifty years old, and it contained just me and a cat named Lydia. I was excited about not teaching anymore, and about getting away from this place, and about summer, so I drew up a long list of things to do—picking berries, hiking, visiting a certain used bookstore that was in a barn, etc.—and then I promptly spent most of the summer doing nothing but sitting around the house, taking daily bike rides out on the college's farm—the only local landscape that reminded me of the Midwest—and cooking dinner for myself every night.

In the middle of the summer, my friend Laura visited me. She and I had been best friends in college, and for two years of graduate school we were a couple, and now we were just friends again. We spent part of our visit walking around campus and revisiting our haunts and talking about our friends. And that was good, being with someone who remembered the same ghosts that I did, someone who reminded me that they weren't ghosts at all, of course, but real people who had simply scattered—mostly to Manhattan and Brooklyn.

Then, later in the day, back at my house, I asked Laura what she wanted me to cook for dinner. She had lived with me for two years, after all, and knew the kinds of things I was best at cooking. And she said, without a moment's hesitation, "Beans and cornbread."

Black Beans for One

Is it soup or just beans? Neither and both, I suppose. Serve it hot, over split cornbread or with rice. For extra goodness, stir shredded cheese into the hot rice before serving.

MAKES TWO SERVINGS (tonight's dinner and tomorrow's lunch)

1 tablespoon olive oil
1 small onion, chopped
1 clove garlic, minced
1 15-ounce can black beans
Salt and freshly ground black pepper

In a medium saucepan, heat the olive oil over medium heat, then add the onion and garlic. Cook them, stirring frequently, until they've started to brown. Add the beans and their liquid, stir, and lower the heat.

Simmer the beans, partially covered, stirring occasionally, until the liquid thickens a bit and is smooth—about 20 minutes. Add salt and pepper to taste. At this point, the beans can be served immediately or removed from the heat, covered, and kept warm for up to 15 minutes.

Single Cuisine
AMANDA HESSER

Tad had gone to Vermont for an annual golf outing. He and a dozen friends play thirty-six holes a day, eat too much beef teriyaki at a bad restaurant called "Vinny's" and go to bed at nine. Not my idea of a good time, but he likes it.

Our apartment seemed hollow without him. Already I had grown used to seeing him reading at our dining room table when I came in from work. I had come to love when our hands bumped reaching for the toothpaste at the same time, and the sound—clink!—of him setting a pan of milk on the stove for our morning coffee.

One day while he was away I was working at home and was having a difficult time focusing. The restaurant that I had reviewed had changed its menu just before publication and I was struggling to get another story to unleash itself onto the page. For hours, I clicked back and forth between e-mails and a blank screen.

For a change of pace I went out on our deck to water the flowers. I heard rustling below, where our garbage cans are kept.

Our garbage had recently been ransacked and our bank information had been used in a scam. So I leaned over the railing to take a look. A man was lifting a bag of our garbage from the can.

"Hey you!" I shouted. "Hey, you! I see you picking our garbage!!"

The man turned and looked up at me. "What's that, m'am?" he said.

"I *said*, I caught you picking our garbage. Now get out!!"

"Oh, miss. Are you the new tenant, Ms. Amanda?"

"Yes," I said, warily. I now noticed that he was neatly dressed in jeans and a fitted polo shirt. "Why?"

"Oh, hello. I'm Gilbert," he said with a French Caribbean lilt. "Welcome to the neighborhood!"

Gilbert, I knew, was the man who has taken care of our building for years. But we hadn't yet met.

"Thank you. Nice to meet you," I said, and slunk inside.

Thoroughly humiliated, I definitely could not write. So I did the only thing I knew would relax me: I went grocery shopping. I walked slowly through the aisles of our local gourmet store, Garden of Eden, taking in bottle after bottle of olive oil, the neatly stacked tins of anchovies and sardines, and the display of cheeses. I picked up eggs and a long loaf of bread. At the greenmarket nearby, I bought garlic chives, fresh figs and a head of butter lettuce that was as tight as a fist. As I shopped, it occurred to me that the menu I was dreaming up was nothing I would ever cook for Tad or for friends. It was less structured and more self-soothing—separate entities tied together by nothing more than the fact that I liked each part. With anyone else, I would feel obliged to make a meal with a beginning, middle and end, a meal that would cohere.

There was nothing guilt-making about the foods I had chosen. They were simply flavors and textures that I love.

My habits are not eccentric. I know many women who have a set of home-alone foods. My friend Aleksandra, for instance, leans toward foods that are white in color. Her signature private dish is polenta. "I cheat and use the five-minute kind," she says. "But I cook it with a broth made from porcini bouillon cubes. When the polenta starts to form a mass, I add a splash of heavy cream and some Parmesan. If I have truffle butter in the house, I add that. If not, I drizzle the polenta with white truffle oil, off the heat. If I want something really mild—and white—I cook the polenta in milk instead. It is like breakfast, that way, but better. If I were rich, I'd use white truffles and shave them copiously over the polenta. Or maybe I'd wait for John."

Aleksandra also makes grilled cheese sandwiches with Gruyère and a sprinkling of white wine (before broiling), sliced comice pears sautéed in butter and sugar, coconut sticky rice, pasta with "just a little butter, Parmesan and black pepper," and before bed, a mug of hot milk sprinkled with freshly grated nutmeg.

My own sister, Rhonda, favors things like rich cheeses, fried chicken, and goose liver pâté on toasts. Her specialty is spaghetti with fried eggs. She fries two eggs and a clove of garlic in oil while she boils spaghetti for one. When the pasta is done, she puts it back in the pot, drops the eggs on top and showers it all with pepper and grated cheese. Then she tosses it with a little pasta water and as she does, the egg yolks crack open and dress the strands of pasta, making it like a rustic, simple carbonara, minus the bacon.

Ginia, a friend from work, has created a dish, which she calls, jokingly, "single girl salmon." She simmers tiny green French lentils and seasons them with white wine vinegar, lemon juice, salt and pepper. She fries shallots with a dash of sugar until they're caramelized, then sautés the salmon. The dish gets layered like an entrée at Union Square Café, and she even garnishes it with parsley. It is a model for all single women because it is at heart about taking the pains to treat yourself well.

Another woman I know says that even if she orders in, she always sets her table with a place mat, china, silverware and linen napkin. I have a similar ritual. I do not eat standing up, and I do not watch television. And when I cook I refuse to use more than one pan. A great meal alone is joyous but ending it with a lot of dishwashing diminishes the effect.

My home-alone dinners are often composed of one or two flavors, prepared in a way that underlines their best qualities. Eggs are high on the list. I rarely eat breakfast but I adore eggs and there are very few opportunities to eat them at other times of day. So I might poach one and lay it on a nest of peppery or bitter greens. I might toss a poached egg with pasta, steamed spinach and good olive oil, and shower it with freshly grated nutmeg and cheese. Or, I might press a hard boiled egg through a sieve and sprinkle the fluffy egg curds over asparagus.

It's not traditional comfort food, but it works for me. I like rich, full flavors paired with clean bitter ones—a gentle lull and a bracing finish. I might boil pasta and toss it with grated cheese, nutmeg and butter, and follow up with a baby arugula salad. When artichokes are in season, I will steam one and dip its leaves one by one into homemade mayonnaise. It's a messy, time-consuming dish to eat, but no one is there to fidget. I am the cook, waiter and dining companion.

In the winter, I have made hearty salads of smoked mackerel and red-skinned potatoes and accompanied them with braised leeks. I like to sauté sausages and eat them with a mound of broccoli rabe, a lemon wedge and olive oil; and assemble platters of prosciutto, mortadella and duck liver pâté with a tuft of pars-ley and caper salad. I might roast carrots and beets, and dip them into ricotta seasoned with olive oil and sea salt.

Dessert is a must. Sometimes I'll buy a Pithivier or cherry and almond tart, or toss peaches with sugar and sour cream. I might have cookies, and I am a sucker for caramel ice cream. But my preferred dessert is a bar of dark bitter chocolate and a glass of Cognac.

This night, I was looking for foods to soothe my embarrass-ment about Gilbert. I had been daydreaming about the truffled egg toast from 'ino, a paninoteca in Greenwich Village. It's a thick piece of white bread blanketed under a layer of gently cooked eggs and a cloud of truffle oil. I dropped a nugget of but-ter into a sauté pan the size of a saucer. I whisked a few eggs with a little crème fraîche and poured it into the pan. Then I began stirring it over low heat, stirring in circles and zig-zags and figure eights. The eggs warmed and turned a lemon yellow on the edges.

I remembered a story I once did about making scrambled eggs with Daniel Boulud. He prepared his in a double boiler, whisking the entire time, so that the eggs became more like a custard than like any scrambled eggs I had ever seen. They were extraordinarily delicate. I like to treat myself well, but as I mentioned, I do have a one-pan rule. I wasn't about to pull out my double boiler. My effort to improvise was working fine, anyway. The eggs, with patience, formed into fluffy curds. I put a slice of bread in the oven to toast, and when the eggs were ready, piled them on top of it. I sprinkled on the truffle oil and then let it sit for a minute so the heat from the eggs would moisten the bread.

I left the butter lettuce as whole ruffly leaves and turned them in a bowl with sliced garlic chives and a gentle dressing. I poured myself a glass of pale yellow Fino sherry; the glass began to sweat instantly in the summer heat. The toast calmed my nerves. I carefully ate my salad, carving the leaves into manageable pieces. I heard a door shut outside but otherwise it was silent.

I'd had so many meals like this since I moved to New York. Sometimes they were glorious feasts. Sometimes they were a chore; I would force myself to cook to fortify my independence and to commit to a satisfying life on my own. From now on, they would become an infrequent occurrence. I would miss the dinners, but not life alone.

For dessert, I dropped a spoonful of *dulce de leche* over vanilla ice cream and placed an orange zest cookie on top as if it were a *tuile*. Then I went out on my deck and ate it with a small spoon. I couldn't duck Gilbert for the rest of the time we lived here, I thought. I should bake him cookies or a cake to apologize. I'd ask Tad about it. He was coming home in the morning.

My last night home alone as a single woman was nearly over. The next time I would be married.

. . .

DINNER FOR YOU,
WHEN THERE'S NO ONE TO SHARE IT WITH

Truffled Egg Toast
DINNER FOR 1.

1 teaspoon butter
3 eggs
1 teaspoon crème fraîche
Sea salt
1 slice country bread (not too chewy, not too sour, but sturdy)
White truffle oil

1. Melt the butter in a tiny skillet over very low heat.
   Whisk together the eggs and crème fraîche. Season
   with salt. Pour this into the skillet and use a whisk
   or wooden spoon to stir it, making sure to cover
   the entire bottom surface. This will take at least 10
   minutes, so be patient. If you do it too fast, the egg
   will dry and the curds won't be as silky. Toast the
   bread and put it on your favorite dinner plate.
2. As soon as the eggs have formed soft curds and
   are loose but not raw, spoon them onto the toast.
   If some of the egg tumbles off, that's fine. Sprinkle
   with truffle oil, and let sit for a minute before
   digging in. (Eat with a fork and knife.)

Single Girl Salmon
ADAPTED FROM GINIA BELLAFANTE

A FINE FEAST FOR ONE. DOUBLE IT IF YOU HAVE A GUEST.

Ginia came over one night to show me how she makes this dish, a marvelous confluence of salmon, lentils and shallots. Tad was home, too. We stood close by with glasses of rosé in hand as she went to work, chopping shallots, peeling garlic, tipping lentils into a pan. She moved quickly, like a line cook who was dressed like a model, in heels and a vintage dress. Ginia is a fashion writer.

"One of the reasons I like this dish," she said, "is that it's so easy. One garlic clove, one shallot, one bay leaf, one piece of salmon."

"It's like a pound cake," I said. Pound cakes are always even proportions of butter to sugar to flour.

She began by simmering lentils, and when they were done, she seasoned them with an alarming amount of salt. "You can never have enough salt," she said. "Vinegar, too. I sometimes add lemon juice as well, to create a complex acid." She's no slouch when she's alone.

Next she sautéed coarsely chopped shallots in a pan with oil and sugar, stirring vigorously as if she were washing a window. When the shallots were done, she returned the pan to the stove.

She turned to me: "What happens now is the following: we stick in our little salmon friends and then we sear them at a high heat so we can get the skin off." Ginia has made the salmon often enough to fine tune it. Salmon renders a lot of fat and the skin just gets in the way, so she figured out a way to quickly render the fat and then swiftly scrape up the skin, leaving the salmon to finish cooking. She could ask for skinless fillets, but then she wouldn't have enough fat to fry the salmon. This way, the fat serves as a cooking medium and the skin protects the fish for most of the rigorous sautéing.

When the salmon was done, Ginia laid it on top of the lentils and began layering shallots, parsley and a generous squeeze of lemon juice. The lentils were bright with acidity, the salmon was sweet and that sweetness was echoed in the shallots. Tad and I toasted Ginia, then dug in.

⅓ cup tiny green French lentils

1 clove garlic

1 bay leaf

Sea salt

Freshly ground black pepper

2 tablespoons olive oil or walnut oil

1 tablespoon white wine vinegar

1 tablespoon lemon juice

1 large shallot, chopped

Pinch sugar

1 7-ounce fillet salmon, cut from the center (ask to have a
    square piece, rather than a skinny slice)

1 teaspoon chopped flat-leaf parsley

Lemon wedge

1. Rinse the lentils, then pour them into a small saucepan with the garlic clove and bay leaf. Cover with water (about ½ inch above the lentils). Set a lid on top, slightly askew. Bring to a boil, then adjust the heat so it is at a simmer. Cook until the

lentils are just cooked through but still have a little bite, 15 to 20 minutes. Ginia does hers so they are like firm peas or al dente pasta.

2. Drain the lentils and put them in a bowl. Season generously with salt and pepper. Pour in 1 tablespoon of olive oil, the vinegar and the lemon juice. Fold and stir the lentils for a minute, so the seasonings blend well, then taste them. They should be quite tangy, because salmon is fatty and you will need something to sharpen it up. Ginia continued tasting the lentils every few minutes and adding more lemon juice as she prepared the shallots and salmon.

3. Place a small skillet over medium heat. Swirl in the remaining 1 tablespoon of olive oil and add the shallots. Drop in a pinch of sugar, then stir as the shallots cook, turning them over and over, until they're soft and have a glazed and golden look. Transfer to a plate and place the pan back on the stove over medium-high heat. Season the salmon with salt and lay it skin-side down in the pan. Let it cook for 1 minute. It will begin to render its fat and the skin will crisp and stick to the pan. When it is crisp, use a spatula to scrape up the skin. Ginia scrapes it up, quickly turns the fish and removes the skin from the pan. This may take one or two tries the first time around. Continue sautéing until the salmon is cooked on the edges and

has just a thin line of pink running through the center.

4. To serve, spoon the lentils onto a plate. Lay the salmon fillet on top, and dab on the shallots. Shower with parsley and squeeze over a wedge of lemon.

Asparagus Superhero

PHOEBE NOBLES

Last spring, I ate asparagus every day for two months. I turned into a superhero of asparagus.

In my secret life, I was the *Spargelfrau*. Perhaps it wasn't the right name for a superhero. I got it from an article a friend sent me about asparagus season in Germany, which happens there at roughly the same time it happens in Michigan—May through June. The article said some German villagers get so excited about their asparagus, they eat it every day while the season lasts.

The *Spargelfrau*, I think, is actually supposed to be the woman who *sells* asparagus, not the one who buys it all up and eats it. (It strikes me now that *Spargelfrau* could mean *wife of asparagus*. I don't know if domestic union with a vegetable merits a pair of Underoos.)

In some famous little asparagus town in Germany, there is a statue of the *über-Spargelfrau*, fat cheeked and grinning, a sort of wholesome vixen. She has a cart on wheels. She is holding armfuls of bronze asparagus.

Surrounded by bushels of real greens in an open market, the

Spargelfrau makes a charming newspaper photograph. But I picture her there, in the town square in winter, covered in snow, holding that dead, cold asparagus out to nobody. Poor *Spargelfrau*. In real life, asparagus heroism is temporary. It is intense. There is a great deal of asparagus all at once. The hero must ingest this—raw! steamed! roasted! grilled!—and then, abruptly, stop. There are no memorials. By July the heroism must be forgotten in an orgy of peppers, summer squashes, pole beans. Nowhere in the world should there be asparagus in winter.

The winter in Michigan is long, dark, and damp. There are three things you can get fresh here year-round: beef, bread, and beer. Everything else comes from far away. Everything else, in winter, comes from a Sysco truck, along with millions of Styrofoam coffee cups. If we lived close to the land, Neander-Michiganders, we would hoard potatoes. As it is, we import vegetables, pulpy and withered.

But who needs them? The weather, perhaps like winter somewhere in Germany, makes you *want* nothing but beef and beer. If you know what you are doing in a Michigan winter, you will greet depression with depressants. Pad your dying soul with flesh. Give up and get fat. Hibernate. In the impossible spring, your cheeks will be round enough for the right *spargel* grin. A grin worthy of the triumph of cathedral tips breaking through the ground: *the asparagus is here!*

The asparagus is *all* that's here, in the farmers' market in May, aside from a few stalks of rhubarb. We are still wobbly on our indoor legs. Under our eyes are deep circles of leftover winter despair. We have been waiting so long for a vegetable or fruit. The spring equinox back in March was irrelevant, cruelly crafted for a lower latitude. We started thinking of strawberries when we saw the first crocuses killed by frost, but that was a pipe dream. The strawberries still aren't quite ripe—but when they are, they will be dark and concentrated, almost as if they've had to furrow their brows.

Michigan is a place, for me, of two firsts: living alone—well, *this* alone—and depending heavily—*this* heavily—on the seasons. Before I moved here, I couldn't avoid the fact that I lived in an international pleasure dome—New York City.

I shopped at the Greenmarkets as much as I could. I kept up with the slight seasonal differences between Jersey tomatoes and upstaters, and distrusted calendar-defying hydroponics. Often, especially at Union Square, there was overwhelming bounty. I always liked a tiny Greenmarket for providing a challenge or imperative: *oh, it's only the tomatillo people today.* Given the overdose of choice in the global-capitalist world, I normally have a hard time deciding what to cook. But here—tomatillos. I would have to make salsa. On assignment.

The dawning and dwindling ends of the growing season are also good for imposing menus. There might be only radishes and arugula in the early spring. In fall there are nothing but oven fillers: long-cooking squashes and apples that eventually give way to warty gourds and Christmas wreaths.

But even though there are real farms and farmers in the regions around the city, New York defies reliance on the season. When pickings were slim in the winters I lived there, I just bought pineapples and papayas at the Korean deli. I could get these at midnight if I wanted to. The growing seasons of the rest of the world were ours. Eating local in New York City can mean eating mung-bean sprouts that have arrived from somewhere far away via Chinatown, or fishing a cake of tofu out of your local deli's tofu water.

Of course there are supermarkets where I live now. I buy bananas. I buy lemongrass and cilantro. I don't stop myself from trying (usually failing) to get a good fig, even if you can't grow one anywhere near here.

But, partly because I don't have a car, the easiest and most satisfying place for me to shop is at the farmers' market. I can walk there. And in summer, the Michigan crops—cherries, corn, eggplants, leafy greens, tomatoes, blueberries, apricots, squashes— are miraculous. In late fall, though, I fail to make the shift to the supermarket, with its Chilean grapes, its Texan greens. I keep going to the farmers' market even when there is almost no food. From November through April, I wander under the corrugated shed roof, along the walkways where farmers huddle by portable heaters on Saturday mornings to sell apple fritters and cider. We greet each other with mutual suspicion—*what are you doing out here?* In our eyes is a lean and hungry vegetable craving. In our cheeks is apple doughnut, our serving of fruit and fiber and happiness for the day.

So, even if you don't like asparagus, you can understand the thrill of seeing those bundles of slim stalks standing upright on the tables early one Saturday morning. It's still chilly out. Maybe you haven't had your first cup of coffee. But the asparagus tips sparkle, in your green-starved eyes, like jewels. Their live green is more alluring than money.[1]

The only reason you don't like asparagus is that you have eaten it in the winter. You have eaten it cooked to olive green. The stalks were fat and woody. In your mouth, an inner slime spurted out of an unchewable skin. Some of this skin you removed from between your teeth like dental floss.

The real spring asparagus is picked at dawn, if you are very lucky, and driven here in just thirty minutes in crates. Take the most slender stalk from the rubber band. You can bend it into a full arc, but still snap it crisply just above the base. The tip is like a baby's ear, sheathed in the slightest fuzz. The stem is luminous with moisture, as if it might ooze a drop from its center. Eat it raw, right away, first thing in the morning. There is only a hint of astringency left on your teeth.

The asparagus superhero feels, at this moment, that she could eat all her asparagus raw for the rest of the spring. But there is going to be a lot to eat. Eventually, so as not to go crazy (though she wears an aura of craziness already; though the craziness is part of the wonder of spring), she will have to diversify. She will have to find recipes.

Shopping for one at the farmers' market, especially as the season goes on and the vegetables multiply, can be a challenge. Farmers want to get rid of a lot in a little time. They'll be packing up by two o'clock. They'll give you a bargain if you take two for

---

1. For the purposes of this essay, all asparagus will be green. What is white asparagus? It is grown in secret caves, as mushrooms are. It is a long, spooky fungus. It is naked and phallic. At the end of winter, I want to see green. White vegetables do not make me want to live.

five, or three for eight. They'll make a baker's dozen. They'll sell
a peck. They grew this for you. They don't come here every day.
How can you insult them by trying to buy single servings? The
bounty of the land does not come in single servings.

At the farmers' market, I shop for a whole family. I live and
cook alone.

The *Spargelfrau* comes home with enough asparagus to feed
a sumo wrestler. On no day of the week will she be so ungrateful
as to leave it off the menu. She wraps the bottoms of the stalks
in a wet paper towel to keep them springy in the refrigerator.

The spring of superheroism really took off when I went with
Rodger, the chef at a local restaurant—where I also worked—to
pick asparagus. He was trying to establish relationships with
farmers so that he could gradually shift the restaurant to local,
and when possible organic, produce. One of his main sources for
asparagus was the field of a dirt farmer who let the community
come and harvest his asparagus crop—it was an old field that
wasn't worth his efforts, in comparison to selling dirt. So Rodger
took crews of his friends and restaurant staff to pick enough to
serve hundreds of people. Rodger counted the number of boxes
we had filled with asparagus and left some money in a coffee can
behind the barn.

Asparagus grows on a complex root system. It is difficult to
plant, easy to harvest. The stalks stick up from the ground and
snap off in your fingers right where they should, at the end of
tenderness. We should have been there in the morning, when
dew clings to the plants, but we didn't make it there until the far

side of noon. The day had turned sunny and parched. The sun, somehow, made the stalks hard to see, playing tricks as it does on a highway mirage. The field appeared to be almost empty. Others had been there to pick only a couple days before, but there was still a deceptive amount of asparagus in the field, standing upright, unprotected. We worked along the rows, stooping, snapping, making piles. After a while, the process turned hallucinatory in the bright sun—one moment I couldn't see any asparagus; then, suddenly, I could see *nothing but* asparagus.

"Have you eaten any yet?" Rodger called from his row. I had been too reverential, attempting some kind of professionalism. I bit into a stalk. It was sweet and delicate and clear.

My one day of contact with the vegetable at its source drew me deeper into its thrall. What is the opposite of kryptonite? I was fueled to almost dangerous levels by the green stuff. Or—is Popeye a superhero?—maybe this vegetable was my special spinach, without the can. My next few meals were made of asparagus I had picked myself. But it was clear that as long as *anyone* was still out there picking, I'd go on eating asparagus.

Steaming is next up from raw on the ladder of asparagus evolution. Some people buy tall, awkward steamers just for asparagus. The stalks stand upright in a perforated cylinder, steaming from the bottoms up so that each piece is evenly cooked. Even though I was about to eat asparagus every single day for two months, I did not want one of these things. What would I do with such an implement for the rest of the year? It would taunt me like a fondue pot. I don't mind the variations in tenderness that mishmashed steaming can produce. I just leave the bottoms a little raw if need be, or, if I'm making something with broken asparagus, throw the tips in the pot a little later than the stems. The delight of asparagus from the market is that you'll never get a bundle of such uniform thickness that you could cook it quite all the same anyway.

Tender, local spring asparagus cooks in a couple of minutes. The danger of steaming asparagus is letting it get too watery to hold on to its sauce—sometimes the butter slides off, the lemon dilutes. Steamed asparagus can sink into a puddle on the plate. It seems to me that it might be more useful, though I have never tried it, to have an upright serving dish than an upright steamer, so that the asparagus can continue to drip dry at the table. Then you could take a piece at a time with your fingers (like toast from one of those English toast racks, which seem to exist only to make the toast cold), dip it in a dish of salt or a cup of melted butter, or rub it along your lemon wedge.

Asparagus is finger food. When I eat at home alone, almost everything is finger food. But even if you are in company, my great-aunt Lonnie assures me that the only polite way to eat asparagus is to pick it up.[2] Have you ever tried to fork a whole stem, and then, if you succeed, to aim the asparagus tip at your

---

2. I have since found that Emily Post says, "The ungraceful appearance of a bent stalk of asparagus falling limply into someone's mouth and the fact that moisture is also likely to drip from the end cause most fastidious people to eat it—at least in part—with the fork." Her limp, dripping—possibly canned—asparagus makes me shiver.

mouth while your tines are stuck in the base, six inches or so away? It's a game of depth perception. The stalk dangles, dodges, then smacks you in the face. And unless you are eating with a steak knife, nothing cuts into a stalk of asparagus as well as your teeth do. A regular dinner knife just bruises it.

I sat with Aunt Lonnie at a luncheon where we had to hold our plates on our laps, perched on the edge of a sofa. There was no way to saw at the food on our knees, but Aunt Lonnie said she would have picked up the asparagus no matter where she was sitting. "Go ahead," said Lonnie as my sister and I hesitated. Despite her benediction, there was something sneaky about eating with our hands in society. And Lonnie, ninety-some years old, giggled a little as we all bit into our stems.

The single person, if he is concerned, as I am, about plowing through his leftovers to avoid confrontations with rotten produce, must create multiple variations on the single ingredient, or repeat themes. A head of lettuce or a bell pepper stretches beyond one meal. A loaf of bread lasts from sandwich to toast to French toast to croutons. After the first night's meal, the bundle of asparagus still stands, a small army in the fridge.

After steaming comes roasting.[3] Roasted asparagus is a triumph, because you can sort of caramelize—I think that is what is happening—whatever vegetable sugars are in there. The tips turn brown and sweet like chicken wings. You cut the slipperiness. You can seal in the salt and pepper and olive oil while the

---

3. See Claude Levi-Strauss, *The Raw and the Cooked.*

asparagus cooks, so you won't need the sauce that was sliding off before. The skin crinkles a little, like a grilled rather than a boiled hot dog—without all the liquid, the flavor is intense.

By June, it starts to get too hot for even the superhero to turn the oven up to 450. I move the asparagus to the grill. This involves threading stalks of asparagus onto three skewers until I have built a kind of raft that rests on the grill without falling through. Some of the asparagus stalks are too thin to be pierced this way. Inevitably, something about the precarious arrangement fails. Stalks fall onto the coals and shrink into sparklers. Some stay on top but blacken. The few that survive make it worth the effort.

I keep eating. I don't know what nutrients are in asparagus, but I am infused with them. I ride my bike and plant herbs outside. To be this happy in Michigan borders on insanity. Yes! The old winter depression bordered on insanity too. Living in a place of lesser contrasts, how would you know what it feels like to come back from the dead?

I steamed, I roasted, I grilled. I was not tired of it yet.

There was no particular reason, after a while, for my determination to eat asparagus every single day it was in the market, except that I had been doing so since the beginning and was assuming the pride of a challenge. By June, there were other vegetables in the market. I could have quit. But I wanted to be *Spargelfrau.* Sometimes, eating alone, you are humble. Sometimes, though, the reason to go through with cooking for yourself is the chance to brag about it afterward. When I talked to my ex-boyfriend on the phone, we would recount meals we had made for ourselves—*see, I live pretty nice on my own*. The asparagus thing was more of a party trick.

Perhaps I should have admitted from the beginning that there is something I love about asparagus aside from the miracle of spring, and even aside from its deliciousness: I love the pee. Nothing seems to redeem the workings of the digestive system like asparagus. It's another verification, after a long winter, that I am alive. Natural processes are working! In fact, what the human digestive system and asparagus do to each other, each proclaiming itself, seems downright heroic.

I have heard the pee is genetic: some people get it, some people don't. The first bite of that first stalk of raw asparagus was all it took for me. The pee smells like absolutely no other pee. It almost smells good. And it always makes me feel redeemed. This is the pee from a healthy vegetable! Beet pee, on the other hand, is always alarming—I never *remember* that I have eaten the beets, and I think I am dying—and coffee pee makes me suspicious, as if the coffee has stripped all the minerals from my insides and dumped them, like a whole bottle of vitamins, out at once.

Despite my airing of it here, digestive processing of asparagus is an intense personal experience. You should enjoy it alone. Some things you should make sure to eat together with people— garlic, sardines. Your breath will smell, your hands will smell, you will exude a special kind of sweat, and it will all be wonderful if your friends are doing it too. But you can eat asparagus all alone and then socialize without fear. Kiss whom you like. The pee (I hope) is yours alone, unlike your breath or your sweat, which you can't help but share.

In fact, too many people should *not* eat asparagus together.

When I worked at a restaurant during the height of asparagus season, when every employee was eating some form of it for their meal, the unisex staff bathroom was impenetrable with a kind of asparagus fog.

The superhero starts to flag in her determination. Asparagus season is as long as Lent. I have to fool myself by not making asparagus the main, plain ingredient. After all, I remember, it's supposed to be a side dish. Those evil supermarket asparagi sit around all winter waiting for someone to overcook them and leave them in a puddle next to a Kroger pork chop.

I can disguise the asparagus by cutting it up in bits and tucking it into things. Leftover cooked asparagus goes into omelets and frittatas. I hide asparagus underneath Gruyère on toast. I sneak it into risotto with lemon and Parmesan. I make it into soup with cream and tarragon. I put it in pasta with garlic and anchovies. I eat it in bites that alternate with bites of hardboiled egg.

As fussy as you might get with asparagus recipes, the superhero has some limits. Stop at hollandaise sauce—there's always too much of it. Nor is it superheroic to wrap asparagus in prosciutto. It insults both the prosciutto and what's inside it. That kind of food is made to impress people—not that a heap of asparagus isn't good with a heap of prosciutto.

But now there is solid good weather and a variety of produce. I have come back to life, and I am forgetting my gratitude for the vegetable that summoned me from the dead. Will I ever be able to pee again without forcing a reprise of my meal into my head? Is there anything new I can do with this stuff? In late June,

I start to hate asparagus. My body is desperate for nonasparagic nutrients. The superhero skips a day. Two days. The superhero crumbles, forsaking her old fuel.

But then, on the tables of the real *Spargelfrau* in the farmers' market, the bunches start to fatten and then to dwindle. I am penitent. It is going to disappear, and I am going to miss it for another ten months. I buy from this last burst of asparagus, pay homage, cooking it so that it shines alone, roasted in olive oil and salt and pepper, with just a little lemon over it.

And thankfully, it is gone. Mirage or no, there is not a stalk left in the field. There is so much in the market—eggplants, carrots, beets, bell peppers, red and blue and brown potatoes, fade-to-white leeks—that I don't have to champion any one thing at all—until the fall, when I will be the Empress of Pears.

HOW TO BE AN ASPARAGUS SUPERHERO

Begin at the first hint of asparagus in your area.

Pick asparagus in the early morning while it is still dewy, or find people who wake up on dewy mornings and pick it for you. Have some coffee.

Eat the first piece raw. Test your biceps.

Week One: Cook the asparagus unadulterated for as long as possible. Keep some eggs and starches—rice, pasta, bread—around, and just enough meat to use as a condiment, like some bacon or a jar of anchovies.

See how fast you can run, how high you can jump.

Alone or in company, use your fingers.

Have plenty of fluids. Pee regularly.

Tell everyone you never skip a day. Eat to impress.

If you use the grill, make sure to have a steak or a fish to put on it too, so you won't be disappointed when you lose all the asparagus to the coals.

Week Six: Just when you think you cannot be a superhero any longer, break asparagus into bits to hide it inside things.

Week Seven (The End): Roast one last time. Squeeze lemon to finish. Finish.

Thanks, but No Thanks
COURTNEY ELDRIDGE

Listen, truth is, I don't cook. As a matter of fact, I hate to cook, I really do. I mean, I love to eat, I just hate to cook. So I married a man who cooks, and he was an amazing cook—a chef, really. Then again, great chef, lousy husband. Now there's a surprise.

Anyhow, now that I'm alone again, or rather, now that I'm single again, everything my ex taught me to cook turns my stomach. Which is a shame, really: his artichokes with vinaigrette were fantastic. His Israeli salad was a piece of cake. And that other dish . . . what's it called? It's Middle Eastern, and there are numerous variations, but all you need is a can of tomatoes, an onion, a couple eggs, and bread. . . . No, I can't remember what it's called.

Just as well, I suppose, because I can't make those things. I mean, I know how to make them, I just can't bring myself to make anything that reminds me of my ex. Which takes me back to my long history with rice. Rice and sugar. Rice and soy sauce. Rice and beans. Oh, there you go—there's something: my rice and beans are edible. Good thing, too, because that's about all I can afford to eat these days. Honestly, there are days I'm still scraping change for the subway, so, fortunately or unfortunately, cooking is the least of my worries.

You know, the other day, I was eavesreading on the subway, and there was an ad in the paper that said *Get Your Gourmet On*... We're talking *AM New York*, okay? Of course I had to laugh, but this whole fine dining, pop-star chef, Food TV craze, it's gone too far. But what really kills me are these people who say things like, *Oh, I could never live without great food and wine.* And on one hand, I know what they're saying, and I try not to be self-righteous, I really do. But on the other hand, I just smile, thinking, I'm sorry, but... do you know what an *asshole* you sound like saying that? Actually, come to think of it, my ex-husband used to say that. Gee, what a coincidence, huh? *Joke.*

All I'm saying is that we came from completely different worlds, and to be perfectly honest, there was a time that had no small appeal. I was fascinated. I mean, come on—when we started dating, I was working two or three part-time jobs, trying to write, subsisting on a steady diet of Uncle Ben's, and he was a master sommelier with a degree in restaurant management who'd moved to New York to open his own restaurant. So of course we had very different views on the place and importance of food in our lives, that was a given. What I didn't know was just how much food could unite or divide two people.

My husband summed it up in a single question, which I remember him asking while we were standing in that broom-closet-size kitchen on Chambers, shortly after we'd married. And the reason I remember is because I thought it was one of the strangest questions I'd ever heard. Were you raised on *canned food?* he said. And I'm telling you, *the look,* the shudder of disgust that ran up and down his spine as he spoke the word *canned*—obviously, something was wrong, but I had no idea what. I was just like, babe, you know the can opener's the one piece of kitchen equipment that I know how to use.

Seriously, canned food, as opposed to what, not eating? Really, what a *bizarre question,* I thought, and I almost started laughing, but all I said was, Yes, why? And then he just sort of nodded, like, oh, how *in*teresting. . . . We *never* ate canned food in my house, he said, taking his plate into the other room. It sounds trivial, I know, but it wasn't—not to me, at least. Not if you knew the guy and knew how much food meant to him, what it said about a person in his eyes. And basically, I just got *slagged,* whether he meant to or not. So I stood there a moment, feeling confused, then strangely embarrassed of myself, my family. . . . So of course there was nothing to do but mock him, wrinkling my nose and repeating the comment in my snottiest tone: *We never ate canned food in my house.* . . .

Childish, I know: I freely admit that it was completely immature of me. But then again, it did make me feel better, mocking him, much better, actually. And the fact of the matter is that we did eat canned food in my house—and lots of it, too. What, does that make me *low class?* Fine. You know what else? Just for the record, I must have been twenty before I learned that Ragu wasn't spaghetti sauce and iceberg wasn't lettuce.

Yes, I was raised on your standard Monday-through-Friday menu of Shake 'n Bake, Spanish rice, tuna casserole, goulash, and leftovers (aka Fend-for-Yourself Night)—you know, good ol' bang-for-your-buck cooking. Out of a can, yes. I mean, seriously, *what did he think?* I told him we were poor—my family, my mother's family—I'm sorry, but isn't it common knowledge that poor means *canned,* and canned means *food* in a poor family? And you're damn glad to have it, too: that's right. Now shut up and eat.

That was my mother's family, at least, which was your basic small-town Catholic lower-middle-class family of ten. In other words, there was no discussion about *food,* are you kidding? You ate what was put in front of you; you ate everything on your plate; and you never, ever complained. Because any child who complained or refused to eat everything on their plate got their ass beat and sent to bed, hungry. That's Catholicism in my book: it's not the number of mouths to feed, it's the one who's howling, getting their ass paddled at the kitchen table. And everyone else just keeps eating, absolutely.

But of course I would say that: one of the only times in my life I was ever spanked was at the dinner table. I was about three, I guess, and one weekend, my mom made this huge pot of chili— another house specialty, chili and Fritos. And because we were broke, she made enough chili to last a week, and it did. So, by Friday night, five nights later, I'd had enough of chili, and I refused to eat my dinner. Even worse, I sassed off right to her face. *I hate chili!* I said, going so far as to shove the bowl across the table. I mean, it was just your basic bratty kid behavior, right? So I was ordered to sit there until I finished my dinner, which of course I refused to do.

So I sat at the table. And I sat. And I sat. And from time to time, my mom checked on my progress, but of course there was none. Because I had decided I would rather spend the rest of my life at that table than eat another bite of chili. It was a Mexican standoff, all right, a Knee-high Noon, and I knew I was pressing my luck. Oh, hell yeah. I knew, but I didn't care. I wasn't eating that shit.

Finally, a few hours later—and granted, it might have been forty minutes, who knows?—but at some point, my mother asked one last time if I was going to eat my dinner. *Never,* I thought, throwing myself across the table and hiding my face in my forearms, nodding, but she wasn't impressed with my perfor- mance. Keep in mind that I'd never been spanked before—my mother didn't need to raise a hand, considering she had this ter- rifying register of voice that said *Don't . . . fuck with me!* And that was the voice she used. This is your *last warning.* Are you going to eat your dinner? she said, firmly taking hold of my biceps. Double down, right? And I wasn't scared—it was thrilling, actu- ally. *Last warning:* I'd never made it that far! It was the moment of truth, and I said no. *No,* I said, and that was it: snap!

I mean, *she lost it.* Oh, man, she pulled me from the table with such force that I knocked over the chair as she started wailing, paddling my ass. Honestly, if she'd had a wooden spoon, she would've broken it on the first swing. But what I remember most was her hand coming down, that there was just this haywire rhythm to her arm, like she couldn't hit me fast or hard enough, and I remember thinking—no, I somehow remember *knowing* that she couldn't stop hitting me even if she wanted to. When she finally did, I was sent to my room, and we never spoke of it again.

In all fairness, maybe she only spanked me a few times, who knows, but that is definitely how I remember it. So it was a good twenty years before we ever talked about the incident. I'm not even sure how it came up in conversation, I was probably telling her what a terrible, abusive mother she had been all my life. Oh, that's right—I cited the chili beating as but one example, and we started laughing, and then my mom finally told me the rest of the story.

The simple fact was we had no money—I mean, *no money*— no food, nothing. We had absolutely nothing else to eat in the house—no juice, no milk, bread, cereal—and my mom didn't know how she would feed me the next morning, or the next day, or the next. I don't know how she got us through that weekend; I could never ask. So yeah, she lost it. And I'm sure I would have done the same in her position. Which might have something to do with never having wanted to be in her position, but anyhow.

Now my mother is an amazing woman, truly, but she's nothing if not proud. Seriously, it took years of pleading before she allowed me to trick or treat, because she always called it the Beggars' Banquet, and *we did not take handouts.* Good Lord. Anyhow, a few years later, sometime during the late seventies, I can only imagine how difficult it was for her to apply for welfare. Then again, she had a kid, and you do what you have to do.

So we did our shopping at stores that took food stamps, and I was enrolled in one of those programs you see advertised on the subway, usually in Spanish. You know those posters with a picture of a smiling young woman and her baby or maybe just some cute little kid—*such bullshit,* but anyhow. You know what I'm talking about, those posters advertising food programs in which the low income can enroll their kids, so you can be sure your kid gets fed one solid meal a day. Which is usually breakfast, every day before school. At least that was the program I was enrolled in, and it used to shame the hell out of me, slipping out of the cafeteria every morning.

Of course it's ridiculous now, but I used to live in mortal fear that one of my classmates would see me and then the whole school, K through nine, would know that Courtney Eldridge was a welfare case . . . *oh, no*! Yes, I laugh. Then again, looking at it now, it's hard to say who was more proud, my mom or me.

I will say that my mother never encouraged or discouraged me from the kitchen. For better or worse, my guess is she never wanted me to feel the kitchen was my place—not unless I wanted it to be, and I didn't. There were just too many other things I wanted to do. But what I realized early on was that the kitchen was always the easiest place to talk to my mom, if I caught her while she was cooking, and how meditative it seemed, watching her hands chopping and stirring. I used to sit on the far counter, watching her cook, and we'd talk in a way that we never spoke anywhere else. Intimately, I suppose, for lack of a better word.

In fact, the first and only time I ever asked my mother if she believed in God was in the kitchen. I mean, I must have been twenty years old, I'd never been confirmed, my mom hadn't been to Mass in a good twenty years, and I was *still* afraid to ask. It's just one of those things we don't talk about. God and food, yes.

Now my husband, on the other hand . . . My husband was Israeli first and Jewish second, as they say. Secular, in other words. But if you ask me, all that really means is the guy had no problem complaining and no tact when doing so. Needless to say, he was extremely, I daresay violently, opinionated on the subject of fine dining in New York City. Case in point: I had to edit the word *battlefield* out of his business plan, okay? And furthermore, not only was our fine dining completely substandard, New Yorkers didn't know *anything* about great food and wine, in his opinion, and I had no choice but to hold my tongue.

I mean, there was a part of me that balked at what I considered nothing more than typical Eurotrash condescension, but then again, how could I argue? Like I said, when we met, I didn't know my Michelin from Meineke, I'm serious. Whereas my husband's entire life was spent traveling the world, staying at four- and five-star hotels, dining at three- and four-star restaurants, and living a very good life, as he was always the first to point out—well, unless his mother was there to remind him first. In any case, when I said he was a chef, I didn't mean he held a culinary degree from CIA or Johnson & Wales, or any of those schools—what need? He had his mother.

Oh, I heard all about his mother, long before we met, yes. . . . Former actress, former model, semiretired world-renowned food critic—a *gastronomic writer,* to be exact. The only thing I heard about more than his mother, really, was his mother's cooking, because *no one* cooks better than my mother, he always said. And not only had she been teaching him about food and wine since infancy, the two of them had been attending special cooking schools and private classes all over the world since he was in his teens, basically.

So yes, my husband was an unapologetic snob, but not impolite. No, he was always polite in the restaurant, but I always knew what was coming, soon as we stepped out the door. This look would just cross his face, somewhere between rage and asking if the chef ate canned food growing up. But of course it wasn't just the food, it was the entire dining experience: the layout; the decor; the lighting; the service; the menu; the specials; how efficiently the kitchen was running that night; and then, the moment of truth, when the first course appeared. . . .

But his eyes would get straight to work as soon as we set foot through the front door, and he knew his business, he really did. I'll give him that any day. Sometimes, watching him take in a room, it was like watching an artist sketch a nude, the way his eyes darted back and forth, from body to canvas, never still. And sometimes he'd make a comment, offering criticism or praise, or mentioning some restaurant he knew in London or Barcelona or wherever. . . . But that's how he taught me, how I learned the most, just from watching him, really. And I was a quick study— I think so, yes.

Then again, so much has to do with exposure. He took me to all sorts of places I'd never been, restaurants I never could've afforded otherwise. Mostly two- and three-star, but the kinds of places I'd always imagined I wanted to go, until you really got down to it, and I didn't, after all. It used to cause me such anxiety, just trying to figure out what to wear, for fear of drawing attention to myself. And *why I cared*—honestly, that was such a ridiculous waste of time and energy. Really, I don't know what I was thinking. Then again, there were a few instances when my ignorance showed.

Like the first time we went to Danube, when I took my wineglass firmly in hand, pretty much like a beer bottle, I suppose, and my husband kept tapping my hand and wagging his finger at me, No no no. Until I finally said, What? What is your *problem?* I asked, completely fed up, then he leaned forward and whispered over the table, explaining that you hold a wineglass by the stem, not the bulb. I didn't know the proper way to hold my wineglass because no one had ever told me. No one had ever taught me any table manners, to be honest. So I was mortified, of course, but thankfully, there weren't too many of those incidents. And otherwise, his view of wine was this: either you like it or you don't. In fact, wine was one of the few things that humbled the guy. Which was a pleasure in itself, really.

So I decided, well, I guess I'll just tell him what I like. Soon enough, when he'd bring home a bottle of wine that really knocked my socks off, I'd call him at the restaurant, while he was working on the floor, just to tell him so. Some afternoons, he'd rush home for an hour between shifts, carrying an erect briefcase full of new wines. Oooh . . . I'd squeal, running to meet him at the door, and throwing my arms around his neck: Is that a *Blah-di-blah-y-Blah-de-blah,* or are you just happy to see me? Then, before I could lay on the full-court press of my solicitation, my husband would share the retail price, telling me not to get used to it. So, feeling slightly deflated, I'd stiffly remove my arms, telling him that if I wasn't getting used to it, he might want to look into some retail prices of his own.

Anyhow, I'd say, oh, 99 percent of the time, we agreed on wine and just about every restaurant we visited. Then again, the more I learned from my husband, the more restaurants *were* disappointing, actually. And it wasn't long before I started realizing what a snob I can be—I have it in me, I'm afraid. And then some. But the thing is, every time, every single time a word of criticism reached the tip of my tongue, I was torn between how I was raised and who I wanted to be. Which was not necessarily someone who complained in restaurants, but still.

I mean, simply admitting that my food wasn't served hot, when he asked about my entrée, felt strangely disloyal. Like I was leaving my family behind or something—it was just so against the grain . . . what can I say? It's hard to let these things go. Christ, my mother was *forty years old* before she could leave a bite of food on her plate. And I remember the day she told me, because I was so proud of her—it was a milestone in both our lives, really. Because I had to wonder how old I would be before I could do the same.

I'll tell you the turning point, though, the night everything changed for me. I mean, we went out to a lot of restaurants, and I enjoyed them, you know, but I can't say I really cared until the night my husband took me to his favorite sushi joint. Which was the night we became engaged, for all practical purposes, because this was his top-secret joint—I mean, this was a serious commitment. I'm not kidding: the guy wouldn't share the name of this place with *anyone*. But I will, of course, gladly. It's this little spot on the Upper East Side called Sushi of Gari, and I was a bit stunned when we arrived, because the place wasn't much to look at, taking our seats at the bar, while my husband ordered us the chef's special and some sake.

Of course I'd had sushi before, but this . . . Sushi of Gari was nothing less than a revelation. I know that sounds exaggerated, but I'm telling you: the man did things with fish I didn't know were possible, that were just . . . *inconceivable* to me before that moment—every single time, too. Because when you order the chef's special, you're served one piece of sushi at a time, and it's a surprise every course.

And obviously the pleasure of sitting at the bar is watching those gentleman prepare your sushi, which is genuine artistry, not to mention a complete turn-on. You know, I've often heard Anthony Bourdain bandy the word *orgasmic* about, and I'd always roll my eyes, thinking, Well, *no shit*, you're a man: that's a given. But still . . . the chef's special at Sushi of Gari is a culinary multiple orgasm. That said, I must have had twelve courses—honestly, ten, easy—before I finally said no more, thank you. And the only reason, the only reason I quit was because my husband had, and I didn't want to look like a complete pig, even though everyone behind the bar knew exactly what the score was. Even so, I could've gone all night.

Suffice it to say, looking at Gari, standing at the helm, with those dashing streaks of gray hair, looking so handsome, so stern, so, so—*masterful,* it was all I could do, biting my tongue, to keep a postcoital *I love you* from escaping my lips. I'm telling you, it was truly mind-blowing, that meal. On par with any musical, sexual and/or pharmaceutical awakening . . . ugh, I cannot imagine skydiving could be more exhilarating. Then again, the bill will certainly bring you back to earth, but anyhow. Sushi was never the same after that. Actually, nothing was the same after that.

It's true, once you know what's possible . . . Well, like they say, you can't go home again. So I figured the best way out of the jam was to take my parents, right? I mean, *I* certainly don't have that kind of money, so God bless good old Mitch and Cathy for com-

ing to town once a year. My folks, yes, who, like me, also thought
they'd had sushi before. Oh, no . . . *oh no no no,* I smiled, assuring
them with my enlightened nod, if you haven't been to Gari's, you
haven't had sushi, trust me, I said. And they agreed. And now,
every time I speak to my dad on the phone, he always makes a
point of asking about the man, if I've seen him recently, speaking in a tone as though Gari was the one I let get away.

Speaking of, rumor has it that Gari was quite taken with my
mother-in-law. And who could blame him? She's stunning. She's
tall, thin, she's elegant, she's led an incredibly glamorous life, and
she's one of the only women I've ever known whom I'd call regal.
Basically, she was everything I ever thought I wanted to be. Plus
thirty years—but even that. I mean, she made aging look pretty
damn good. Like somewhere you might actually want to be, one
day. And at my age, she was absolutely breathtaking.

Then again, truth be told, I didn't like her at first for the simple reason that she was far more interested in talking about food
than me. Hard to believe, I know, but the woman had no interest
in *me,* whatsoever. It's true: we met uptown, that first night, because my husband and his mother were attending some sort of
food-and-wine-pairing series at some posh midtown locale, organized by some bigwig in the French culinary scene, I don't know
what. The point is, I met them for dinner at a Korean barbecue
joint in the thirties. Which I strongly suspect was chosen because
they allow smoking in a back room, those cunning Koreans.

So there I was, trying to make conversation with my mother-
in-law, asking about the tasting, which was exactly the wrong
question. Because apparently, the tasting had proven a terrible
disappointment, which she then proceeded to talk about on and

off, the rest of the night, and I just thought, what is the big deal? So they served guacamole, and it wasn't even good guacamole. Get over it, lady. Jesus Christ. After we dropped her off at her hotel, my husband asked what I thought of her, and all I could say was, Is she *always* like that? Like what? he said. Does she always talk so much about food? Opening the building door for me, he just nodded yes, pretty much. Ohmygod, I thought, how long is she *staying*?

As it turned out, the joke was on me. Because in the end, my mother-in-law proved a far better teacher than my husband, for the simple reason that she knew how to tell a great story. She was a RADA-trained stage actress and she was so passionate about food that just listening to her was a hell of a lot more exciting and educational than any cooking show I've ever seen. Yes, she was the one who taught me that every meal tells a story, literally and figuratively, and yes, she could talk for hours about famous chefs and famous restaurants and famous meals with famous friends, many of whom are now dead, I'm afraid.

As a matter of fact, my mother-in-law was a close friend of Rex Harrison, and to this day, every time she's in New York, she makes a point of looking up Lady Marcia Harrison. They meet at Petrossian and feast on caviar, *mais bien sûr*. Oh, and by the way, it's pronounced Mar-*see*-uh, not *Marsh*-uh.

But she was no name-dropper, my mother-in-law. Really, she was no more interested in talking about a celebrity than a Parisian vendor who'd been selling her leeks since the 1960s. And of course it wasn't what, it was *how* she described the meals, how lovingly and descriptively and animatedly, all in the hopes that those people and places and meals, that those stories might live on. See, that's what I didn't get at first: that she was just trying to share something with me the best way she knew how. I guess I had so many biases of my own, it took a while for me to see that, but once I did, I finally saw the beauty in looking at the world in that light.

It certainly didn't hurt that she had some pretty outrageous stories, too. Like that one about the time Peter O'Toole visited her in Israel—that was one of the most hilarious, depraved stories she ever told. Oh, sure, he looked harmless, sitting in the back row of the Oscars a few years ago, but I'm telling you, that man is *crazy*. . . . God, she has so many stories I'd love to share, but they aren't mine to tell, you see. Regardless, my mother-in-law was the first person to translate her knowledge of food into a language I could appreciate without any backlash of conscience or fear of betrayal. And I grew to love her very much.

A few months after my husband and I married, she visited and took us to a four-star restaurant to celebrate. So of course calls were made—Christ, even the whole thing with making calls and pulling favors, and I know it's partly Israeli, but even that was so strange to me—we never ask for favors in my family, but anyhow. The kitchen was notified we were coming. And it's quite a scene when one of the most famous chefs in the world steps out of the kitchen and approaches one table to speak to one guest in particular. A few minutes later, the chef leaves, of course, but people keep staring: Who are those people? Are they somebody? Should we know them? Funny.

At one point, my husband stepped outside for a cigarette,

leaving me with my mother-in-law, who was telling me a story; I don't remember which, but I was rapt. So, a few minutes later, my husband returned inside, grinning, and he proceeded to tell us that one of the other guests, a senator, no less, had introduced himself outside—*Ooh hooo*, a senator, she and I said, nudging and winking at each other. We'd had a few glasses of wine by then, obviously. Anyhow, the senator laughed, offering my husband his condolences, assuming that my husband was dining with his new wife and his new mother-in-law. We all got a good laugh out of that. And it was probably the greatest compliment my husband ever paid me.

But it wasn't always like that. A year later, my mother-in-law took us to New Orleans for a long weekend. We left New York in the morning, and that cheap-ass American Airlines didn't even serve a crummy bag of pretzels, so we were *famished* by the time we got to our hotel. Well, naturally, ever the culinary explorer, my mother-in-law wanted the real deal, so we made a bee-line for a famous gumbo joint near our hotel. I was so hungry by the time we sat down, I was shaking, and when our gumbo arrived, it was several bites before I realized I was the only one eating: my husband and his mother had put down their forks almost simultaneously.

When the waitress approached, asking about our food, they both smiled and thanked her, saying it was delicious. But as soon as the waitress stepped away, they began speaking in Hebrew, never a good sign. What's wrong? I asked, leaning forward. Inedible: *gruel*, my mother-in-law pronounced, with a violent shudder. I knew that shudder. Sure enough, my husband agreed, and neither touched their food, which left me in a terrible position.

Waste food and go hungry, or prove myself uncouth? Tough call, yeah. Especially when, a moment later, my mother-in-law surmised, Well, it is slave food, after all. And the first thought that came to mind was *I was born a poor black child. Nothing was ever easy for me.* . . . I didn't say a word. And my stomach growled until dinnertime.

So it's probably not too surprising that I never cooked for my husband—are you kidding, between his standards and my lack of skill? Forget it. And he tried, I'll give him that—the man honestly tried to teach me to cook, at least a few of the basics, but it always resulted in a scene straight out of *The Miracle Worker.* Seriously, I can do a pretty impressive Helen Keller, when cornered, and there was my husband, trying to wrestle me down, all but throwing water on me, forcing a utensil in my hand, and signing spatula: S-P-A-T . . . What's funny is that's much too close to the truth.

Honestly, it was a running joke that eventually became a point of contention. When are you going to cook for me? he'd ask, and I'd say, Soon, soon. . . . And for a good year, two years, I had these wild fantasies of blowing him away with some dish or other, but in reality, I was way too intimidated to cook for the guy. I mean, the one thing I could make with any confidence was tuna casserole, but I knew my husband wouldn't eat tuna casserole—he'd rather starve, I'm sure of it. If he wouldn't eat gumbo, he sure as hell wouldn't eat tuna casserole.

No, I did make something for him once: I baked an apple pie, which I learned from my grandmother, who learned from her grandmother, and so of course I made it from scratch, right down to the lard. I went to the farmers' market for the apples, and Garden of Eden for the best vanilla ice cream I could find—I even made a backup piecrust, in case my first effort failed. But it didn't. No.

I'm pleased to report that my pie turned out beautifully—as a matter of fact, it was *damn good,* or so I thought, licking the knife and squeezing my shoulders, excitedly grabbing two plates. I actually surprised myself, and I was so pleased, so proud I'd finally made something for my husband, handing him his plate, thinking, *one thing.* By God, don't ever let it be said I can't make an apple pie. . . . But I still waited, anxiously, as my husband took a bite, and he nodded that it was good, but he didn't like sweets, he said, setting the plate on his bedside table. That was it, I'm afraid.

The only other thing I knew, that he didn't, was Mexican food. My husband had never been to Mexico; he had no idea what authentic Mexican food was about. I learned to make beans in Mexico, the second or third time I went down for any real amount of time, about ten years ago. And there's nothing to it, really, but like most things, it had never occurred to me to make them myself. But ten years later, I make some mean black beans. Now that's one thing I won't eat out of a can, beans—not even Goya brand, no way. Anyhow, by the time I had the nerve to make Mexican food, even just a couple quesadillas, I didn't care anymore. The marriage was long over.

Stillborn, really.

The one thing that makes me sad is that my mother-in-law didn't have more time to get to know my mother, and vice versa. Because these days, my mother's favorite subjects are food and cooking—and I'm so proud, I really am—because I never had a chance to see her so passionate about anything when I was growing up. By the time we finally had some money to our names— excuse me, by the time *she* finally had some money to *her* name—basically, around the time I left home, I realized my mother loved to cook.

She just turned fifty-five, and they're retiring soon, my parents. My mom's toying with the idea of going to cooking school—not in the hope of becoming a chef, but maybe catering, something like that, she says. And honestly, I don't think there's a chef in the world that could do a better job of feeding a family on nothing than she did when I was growing up. So who knows, maybe she has it in her, but I hope not. Not another chef, Mom—please, no more chefs, okay?

You know, I've been on my own for over a year now, and I still have moments when I feel torn by what I learned while I was married. For example, and I'm ashamed to admit this, sometimes I wonder if I should correct my mom and tell her how to hold her wineglass, but I never do. I mean, she wouldn't take it personally, and she might very well appreciate the tip, but it's not that easy. And *I know* it's proper, but that's just wrong in my book. I'm sorry, I will not correct my mother's manners, it's just not worth it to me.

What's interesting is that I've been reading a lot of recipes this past year—even though I only own two cookbooks, yes. The first is *How to Cook Everything*, which my parents gave me for Christmas two years ago, and which I still haven't read, actually. But the other one, the one I have been reading, is my mother's family cookbook. Aptly titled *The Eldridge Family Cookbook*, conceived by my grandfather, while we were all sitting around the dining table, during a family reunion, back in 1984. And you know what, I've hauled that little book across several continents, the past ten, fifteen years, but I'd never read the damn thing before now, no. I just needed to know it was there.

And it's just a little rectangular spiral-bound book, about eight by five and a half inches, with this white cover that my mother designed about fifteen years ago, with these little fruit and vegetable characters. . . . Never mind what it looks like—that's private. Which is why I never showed it to my husband. And as far as he's concerned, I don't regret that decision one bit, because I knew he would never understand, that he wouldn't even try. As far as I'm concerned, it's just regrettable that I didn't have the confidence to show him, to say, this is mine. This is what I come from. And please try not to wince each and every time you see mention of Campbell's mushroom soup, all right?

You know, there was a part of me that was so defiant, and a part of me that was so ashamed, and I really couldn't say which was which at any given point in time. Maybe that was fascinating to him, too, at least in the beginning. Regardless, I can see it now, how much conflict that caused, internally and externally, but I still don't understand it fully, what happened. Because the thing is, I'm not ashamed of where I come from anymore, not in the least. But I'm no longer married to the man, either. So there it is.

Sometimes, looking back at my marriage, I don't know whether to laugh or cry, really. But it was a great education, and I'll never say otherwise. And in all fairness, I'm still torn, even now. I mean, there's still a part of me that looks back and thinks, wow, I ate at Daniel. Imagine that. The girl who used to look both ways before slipping out of the cafeteria. . . . And then there's a part of me that thinks, Wow, I ate at Daniel. Big fucking deal, you know. But I remember that night, and it was a beautiful night. For once in my life I felt rich and cultured—classy, yes. I felt very, very classy. Whatever else happened between us, he gave me that, and I'm grateful, truly.

But I want a life that has plenty of room for things like Linda Logan's Party Pork Balls, or the infamous Leftover Ham Casserole. *Mmm* . . . doesn't your mouth just water? Wouldn't my ex just gag? You wonder why I've been reading recipes: there's your answer. And mark my words, one of these days, the front page of the *Times* Food Section will have a photo of some delicious-looking steamy creamy noodle concoction with the headline: *This Ain't Your Grandma Jean's Tuna Casserole*. And once again, I'll just roll my eyes, thinking, *you fuckers*. . . . There's just no winning.

Anyhow, a few weeks ago, I came across this recipe called Soda Cracker Pie, which I'd never noticed before. But it was the introduction that caught my eye: "Mother says that this really does taste like an apple pie—it was made a lot during the Depression and the recipe should be saved for posterity." Honestly, until I read that, I'd never seen the poetry, never given any real thought to how much life a recipe can hold—not ours—well, not *mine*, at least. I mean, it's been staring at me all along, and I've missed it this whole time. And that's no one's fault but my own.

So I've been thinking it's probably time I learn to cook a few things. You know, just a few things I'll willingly cook *and* eat—both, yes, that's the trick. I've even got my eye on one of the recipes in my family cookbook, my mother's salsa recipe. She's been making that salsa since I was a kid, and I'll tell you what, the woman makes some damn good salsa for a *huera*. Of course, it's also one of the easiest recipes I can find, but I have to start somewhere, right? And who knows, maybe one of these days I'll actually be able to make something Dan taught me to cook, too—but not today, no. Just not today.

Cathy's Salsa

MAKES A QUART.

 1 large can whole tomatoes (drain off half of the juice)
 1 fresh jalapeño pepper
 1 whole dried red chile or red pepper flakes
 Generous shakes of cumin and powdered garlic—more
   generous on the cumin
 1 cap of vinegar
 Salt to taste

Blend all ingredients in a blender. Place in a small saucepan and bring to a boil. Reduce heat and simmer for 5 minutes. Increase or decrease peppers for desired "hotness" . . . and if you have to, use canned chiles. Serve with flour tortillas.

NOTE: Far and away the best I've found in NYC are called, conveniently enough, Authentic Mexican brand white flour tortillas ($2.99 for eight). They put those disgusting dry white mass-market tortillas to shame. Unfortunately, the only place I know that carries them is Commodities on Second and Twelfth. And I'm happy to share my source, but there better be some tortillas there next time I make the trip. Also, I never heat tortillas in a pan with oil; I always heat them directly over the flame, flipping sides every ten or fifteen seconds.

The Legend of the Salsa Rosa
BEN KARLIN

PART 1 : BY WAY OF INTRODUCTION

I come from America.

It is a land of many wonders, but identifiable culinary tradition is not one of them. Sure, you got your New Orleans and
California cuisines. But they are bastardizations. Riffs at best.
No, like millions before me, I was raised in the great American
culinary blandscape. My mom did her level best with tuna casserole and Chicken Every Way You Can Imagine. We were Jewish,
so throw in brisket and gefilte fish. These do not a tradition
make. If anything, they raise more questions. Questions like: Just
how persecuted were Jews to still feel the need to punish themselves like this?

Nevertheless, from a relatively early age I had a taste for interesting food. I had no hang-ups and even took an unchildlike relish
in eating freaky gross things like *gorgle*.[1] As a reward for good

---

1. Yiddish for chicken neck.

grades in junior high, I asked my parents to take me to the restaurant of my choice. I chose a Korean restaurant that specialized in seafood. I insisted on trying shark fin soup and octopus and squid—common enough now, but in early eighties suburbia virtually unheard of. This was the time before sushi. It was the time all things exotic fell under the command of one General Tso.[2]

My parents' divorce resulted in me living with my dad, who did not cook. This forced me to get comfortable working solo in the kitchen at age fifteen. Early forays included:

1. Microwaving potatoes until they turned translucent and gelatinous. Lesson learned: one cannot *bake* a potato in a *microwave* oven.
2. Boiling rice in a non-Pyrex glass pot and watching it explode all over the kitchen.[3] Lesson learned: exploding glass is scary.
3. Leaving pasta in boiling water for so long, an entire pound of spaghetti fused into a single noodle. Lesson learned: a pound of spaghetti, even if it ultimately becomes one noodle, is too much for one person to eat.

Over time I became a limited but competent cook. My father usually came home too late for dinner, so more often than not I was cooking for one. This worked out great in the event of disas-

---

2. China, c. 534, pre–Sui Dynasty, famed for setting up Eastern Wei Emperor hostile to Chinese culture; also famed for delicious chicken dish.
3. Grains of which would be discovered in an adjacent room five years later, when the house was sold.

ter, because I was the sole victim. But in the event of triumph, it also meant I was the sole victor. For some reason, this tasted bittersweet. I cooked out of necessity. What I wanted was inspiration.

PART 2: AN INTERLUDE TO THE CONTINENT

In the fall of my junior year of college I studied abroad in Florence, Italy, where the foreign exchange student population outnumbers bona fide Italians fifty to one. Still, it was Italy, where lunch means an entire nation shuts down from one until four-thirty. There I ate my first real tomato.[4] In Italy I discovered there were more than three kinds of cheese.[5] I learned the word "tripe" is not necessarily pejorative. And in Italy I was taught the secret of salsa rosa.

Though it sounds Mexican, salsa rosa is very much Italian. Its origin: the grandmother of one of my fellow students in Florence. He was Italian-American. He had a name like Dante and undoubtedly came from southern Italian stock. It was a simple dish, really. Garlic, olive oil, thin-sliced zucchini. A mix of Roma tomatoes—fresh and the Pomi kind that come in the cardboard container. From there, you add insane, heart-stopping amounts of butter, *parmigiano*, and a glorious chunk of fat known as *panna*. *Panna* is semi-solid cream. Think about heavy cream. Then imagine someone saying, "Not heavy enough." This was cream

---

4. Siena, late May, with my mom. Cut it with a Swiss Army knife; juice ran down my arm. I asked her what the hell those red things were we'd been eating all those years.
5. Also that American cheese is not technically a cheese, but a cheese-food product.

that made crème fraîche seem "runny." You squeezed it out of a juice box—and you really had to squeeze. No pouring, for it was not liquid. As you added the cream and the butter and cheese to the tomato base, the sauce would unmysteriously turn pink—hence salsa rosa. Pink sauce. Generously ladled over pasta—spaghettini or cappellini, mainly—salsa rosa induced an eyes-rolling-to-the-back-of-the-head type of ecstasy.

One night, in one of our cheap, cold student flats, we organized a dinner for our Italian language class. Four or five of us took on cooking duties. This consisted of going shopping together, arriving at the apartment early, smoking massive amounts of hash using the famed "hot butter knife/cardboard toilet paper roll" method, and getting down to some brass fucking tacks cooking. Dante served as chef de cuisine, he being in command of the recipe. The response from our fellow students was pure rapture. As for our Italian teacher, Elisabetta, she either enjoyed salsa rosa or was too polite to say otherwise. She had the annoying habit of speaking exclusively Italian. Since it was early in the semester, we were picking up only about 30 percent of what she said anyway. I left that evening, drunk on the power of good cooking, and, of course, drunk on wine.

Here, a lesser writer might surrender to cheap hyperbole, and say something like, "Salsa rosa changed the very course of my life."

Salsa rosa changed the very course of my life.

. . .

I knew, however, that to deliver the goods on my own, I would have to practice. Cue the training montage.

I shopped alone at Florence's famed Mercato Centrale, becoming fast friends with Tomato Woman, Fresh Pasta Lady, and Angry Man Who Sells Zucchini. I had already established a rapport with Sexy Baker Sisters and Impossibly Beautiful Daughter of Wine Seller. My boyish enthusiasm and game attempts to communicate in their language either charmed or numbed them into submission. Either way, they came to smile when I entered their world and they tried their best to advise me.

But in my small, poorly equipped kitchen I did not enjoy their counsel. My uninterested roommates—an obsessed cyclist, an artist just coming out of the closet, and a third dude of such unremarkable bearing, I can remember not a single detail about him, not even a name—were rarely home.[6]

Alone, I tried to replicate the sauce as we'd made it that first night. With nothing written down, I needed to re-create the process by memory and feel. The hardest task was dialing down the portions, since I was going from cooking for twenty to cooking for uno.[7] Was one zucchini too many? Just how many tomatoes could a single person eat? What about garlic—when are you officially offending others with its smell? And then there's the butter, cream, and cheese. Was it possible to give yourself a heart

---

6. To be fair, they probably remember me as "that snobby prick who spent *way* too much time in the kitchen."

7. One.

attack with one meal, or was that something that could only happen over time?

My first attempts were frustrating. The sauce looked weak and watery, then overwhelming, then not salty enough, then poorly balanced. I began to worry. What if, on that magic evening with the Italian class, it wasn't the sauce that was good, but the hash? Would I now have to smoke before every meal? Would I become some tragic Billy Hayes–like character busted at Milan Malpensa with fifteen bricks taped to my chest all because the secret ingredient to a pink sauce was Khandahar Super Gold?[8]

By the fifth or sixth time, with a kitchen now given over to the smell of burnt garlic, I found the salsa rosa groove. It worked in the lab. Now I wanted to see if it would work in the market. My chance came in a matter of days, when some college friends who were studying abroad in Sevilla visited me while passing through Italy. I sent them to the Uffizi to get their art on while I prepared. A few hours later, they were back, sitting, eating, growing more impressed with each bite. It was like I had absorbed some part of Italy by osmosis, while all they had to show for their time in Spain were sangria stains on their pants.

A week later, I made it again, this time for a girl I had been (lamely) wooing. Two months later we were doing it on a train in the Austrian countryside. Thanks, salsa rosa!

The last time I made salsa rosa in Italy was for a good-bye

---

8. That's a made-up name for hash—I really don't know if they name hash the same way they name pot. I mean, I wish I knew that. I imagine a person who knows that has really lived.

dinner for a small group after our program ended. I robotically sliced zucchini in my kitchen, thinking about all the times I had made the dish. I thought about how much better it was now. I thought about my experiments and my experience and why the sauce improved each time I made it. It was a brutal but important lesson for someone who, up to this point, had done far more cooking for himself than for anyone else. I realized the secret ingredient in most great cooking is the confidence of others—the look in their eyes, the nods of encouragement and amazement that what they are eating is so good and you were responsible for it. For me, the proof did not come in the pudding, but in being surrounded by pudding lovers.

PART 3: REVENGE OF THE SITH, AKA A HERO RISES, AKA AND YOU SHALL KNOW ME BY THE TRAIL OF THE SATISFIED

I returned for my senior year in college armed with no discernible plan for the future but in command of a delicious recipe for sauce. I shared an apartment with my two best friends, neither of whom had use for a kitchen, having mastered only ramen noodles and a curious combination of frozen corn, onions, and melted cheese best consumed before passing out with all your clothes on. I was not much better. Turns out, cooking for yourself in Wisconsin isn't nearly as romantic as cooking for yourself in Florence. Not to mention, I had to go back to eating faux-matoes. Our oven lay dormant for long weeks. Perhaps I had just had a passing love affair with cooking. I was in Italy, young, impressionable, with not nearly as many friends as I had hoped for.

About a month into the semester, I decided to try and hustle my way out of the slump. It was early fall in the Midwest— harvest time. The spectacular farmers' market was at its most beautiful, thick with farmers and kind, smelly hippies selling flourless vegan cookies that tasted like potting soil. Though a plucky exporter had yet to realize the genius of bringing *panna* to Madison, Wisconsin, I managed to replicate the recipe adequately enough. I made it first for me, then for others, but I no longer needed to cook for people to appreciate the food. I am not embarrassed to admit that it was during this period I started garnishing the plate even though I was the only person eating.

A few years later, an opportunity arose to go back to Italy. My friend Jeff, a musician, was living in Padua, to the north. He and another American, Jason, had hooked up with a guy named Marco. Together with a drummer named Ugo, they formed a band. I argued the band had to be called Ugo, because it was, to that point, the greatest name I had ever heard. These were rich kids. Not obscenely wealthy, but wealthy enough to be twenty-five and playing in a band that made no money and not have to sweat it. Their days were filled with dizzying amounts of nothing in particular. I would later learn these types of young Italian men were called *i vitteloni*. Fellini made a movie about them. Barry Levinson's *Diner* ripped it off. Or paid homage. Depends who you ask.

One night, feeling bold, I offered to cook for *i vitteloni*. The menu was never in question. It was only a matter of finding the *panna*.[9]

Unless they are apprenticing to be chefs, young Italian men do not cook. They can make themselves a simple pasta with cheese and butter. That is all. They stay nestled in their protective pouch suckling at the teat of mama's cooking until a replacement nipple in the form of a wife comes along. My dinner party would be a one-man operation. By now, that was the way I liked it.

We toasted to being young and trouble-free and then we ate. And it was good. Seconds and thirds were had. Bread was used to wipe away any stray sauce clinging to the bowls. Italian superlatives were tossed around—words like *buonissimo* and *fantastico* and *bravo* and some others that are technically vulgar, but in this context were complimentary.[10] I was overcome with the feeling I imagine actual chefs get from time to time—undoubtedly more at the beginning of their careers, before the jading sets in. You know you have brought great pleasure through the work of your hands and mind. You are a giver of joy. You are a god.[11]

But this feeling was a minor peak, not the summit, for during cleanup I would be paid the highest compliment of my life. Ugo, the drummer, who was rakish with floppy hair, threw his arm around me, and asked me a question that under less manly circumstances would have brought tears to my eyes.

"Ben," he said, "I must ask you, can you teach this recipe to my mother?"

---

9. Now readily available in the supermarket in the Things That Will Kill You aisle.

10. In Italian the word "pig" can be used to spectacularly offensive ends.

11. A lesser god, like Bacchus or Hephaestus, but still a god.

"Yes, yes," the others chimed in. "You must teach our mothers how to make this."

I said, "Yes."

I think. My Italian not being what it once was.

EPILOGUE

I am older now. I happen to be married to an Italian woman. She knows how to cook. She learned from her mother, who learned from her mother, who undoubtedly learned from her mother. I imagine this goes back some time, probably to when they were not Italians but Etruscans. In any case, I'm fairly sure she is directly related to either Romulus or Remus. Once, before we were married, when I was still trying everything in my arsenal to impress her, I told her about salsa rosa. I told her with my chest puffed out.

"So good, it was, they asked *me* to teach it to their mothers."[12]

She laughed, and in her lilting Mediterranean accent brought me low. "That's not even an Italian dish," she said.

"It's from the south," I answered, first words confident, last words not so much.

She looked at me and shook her head. "No, it definitely is not."

"Okay," I said wanly, voice trailing, more like a question. "But it's still really good?"

I didn't even convince myself. Like that, the legend was gone.

---

12. Imagine super-Jewy inflection to maximize *Annie Hall*–like juxtaposition.

Now I no longer make the salsa rosa, not even for myself. It is retired, like Secretariat was before he died, of what I like to think were natural causes.

Salsa Rosa for One

MULTIPLY INGREDIENTS BY TWENTY FOR GROUP PREPARATION

3 tablespoons olive oil

5 cloves of garlic, sliced thin

1 small zucchini, sliced (optional)

3 roma tomatoes, chopped

1 box Pomi diced tomatoes, around 20 ounces

2 tablespoons unsalted butter

⅓ cup *parmigiano* cheese, grated

1 box *panna* (cooking cream), about 6 ounces, or half pint heavy cream

⅓ pound dry pasta (spaghettini, cappellini, or any long thin noodle. Do *not* try with fusilli, penne, or farfalle or you will seriously be fucked)

Salt and pepper, to taste

Heat the olive oil in a medium saucepan over medium heat.

Add the garlic and cook, stirring, until it just turns brown.

Add the zucchini and cook, stirring, until it has a yellowish sheen.

Add the fresh and boxed tomatoes. (Canned whole tomatoes will work too—just make sure there are some fresh ones in there.)

Lower the heat a bit and cook until all the tomatoes start breaking down and forming a *sugo* (sauce).

Now *add* the butter, cheese, and cream, but don't add it in all at once.

Mix it in, so the sauce continues to cook and reduce down. You want to do at least three or four waves.

Once it's all in, set the heat to low and cover.

Boil your water and cook your pasta al dente. Remember, it will finish cooking once it's out of the boiling water, so don't leave it in too long.

After you strain the pasta, *throw* it back into the pot with a nice *pour* of extra-virgin olive oil.

Add some salt and pepper, then *pour* the salsa rosa over the pasta.

Mix, but not too roughly, just so it gets slithery with sauce.

Eat it.

Run a marathon the next day.

Eating Alone

MARCELLA HAZAN

I am probably the first woman from either side of my family ever to have eaten alone. My mother never spent a day or night alone under any of the roofs that sheltered her during her one hundred and one years and four months of life. Nor did her mother, who died at eighty-six. Nor did my father's mother, who lived well into her nineties. My first experiences of eating alone came during the long years of university life at Ferrara, where I took two doctoral degrees in the sciences. I was doing it alone but I could not describe it as serious eating. I was certainly capable of becoming hungry, but when I was young, food as such was at the very bottom of my list of interests. I grabbed anything that I could dispatch quickly and that consumed as little as possible of my minuscule living allowance. It was never anything more demanding of money or time than a *panino* stuffed with mortadella.

My palate came to life when I married Victor, a man whose thoughts were more likely to turn to food than to almost anything else. In my married life, during the years that we spent in

Italy and those in New York, I took many of my meals alone. When we lived in Milan, Victor was often away on location supervising the shooting of the television commercials he had created for McCann-Erickson, the advertising agency where he worked. More than a decade later, when we lived in New York, he was in Italy periodically over several years doing research for the wine book that Knopf eventually published.

Unlike my husband, who loves to dine by himself at a restaurant, if I have to be at a table for one, it has to be at home. When my husband is away, I salivate for chicken because that is the only thing he prefers not to eat. In Italy, it was an easy longing to satisfy. I would pick up a small, freshly roasted chicken at a neighborhood *rosticceria*, buy the makings of a salad—either some *misticanza* (a mixture of wild and domesticated greens) or tomatoes, a cucumber, and spring onions—and a loaf of ciabatta or other good bread. I could hardly wait to get home to enjoy my feast. The first time I tried that in the States, however, I was deeply disappointed. Before they roast a chicken in Italy, they rub it thoroughly with salt, and they put a sprig of rosemary and a clove or two of garlic in its cavity. It is simply delicious. In America, on the other hand, rotisserie chickens have next to no flavor and they are overgrown besides. Once I had discovered this, I enhanced the flavor of the chicken I took home by adding to it the missing salt, garlic, and rosemary and reheating in the oven for fifteen minutes or so. It may not be quite the real thing, but short of cooking one for myself from scratch, which is unthinkable, it is an acceptable imitation.

I adore chicken, but I cannot have it several days running. On the first day, when it is warm, I will have the dark meat, and for the second time around, I will have the breast cold, sliced thin, and moistened with a few drops of very good olive oil. After that, *basta*, enough! We are not accustomed to eating the same thing in succession and we usually do not keep leftovers. If what I have cooked exceeds our appetite, our friends are always willing to relieve us of anything we don't finish. On the exceedingly rare occasions that there are leftovers, I transform them into something different, as I have described in my cookbooks.

The prospect of eating alone will sometimes make me lose interest in food, and when that happens I must turn to the one thing whose aroma and flavor can powerfully jog my appetite: anchovies. I always have very good quality anchovies in my kitchen, which I use in various pasta sauces, or in the Piedmontese vegetable dip *bagna caôda*, or for providing subliminal excitement deeply embedded in the juices of a veal roast. But nothing matches the thrilling intensity of an anchovy fillet laid over a slice of grilled bread slathered with sweet butter. It is blues-chasing flavor so direct that it feels as though you are mainlining it. For that purpose, you need first-rate anchovy fillets packed in olive oil that do not just taste of salt. The best are the extra-large fillets packed by Ortiz, which are not cheap. Another good packer is Agostino Recca from Sicily.

When I am alone, I cringe at the thought of cooking, which I may do only if I have exhausted every other plausible option. The preserved seafoods of the Mediterranean, whether packed in olive oil like anchovies, tuna, or sardines, or dried like *bottarga*, the preserved roe of mullets or tuna, all of them always at hand in my cupboard, deliver many agreeable alternatives to actual cooking. *Ventresca*, tuna's succulent belly, is another of my favorites. I could eat it right from the can, but I don't because I love it in a salad. If I have some cooked cannellini or *borlotti* beans in the refrigerator, I warm them up with some of the liquid they have been cooked in, then drain them and add them to a can of *ventresca* together with several thin slices of raw onion. I toss it with a few drops of vinegar, lots of olive oil, and lots of black pepper. If I don't have the beans, I substitute a very ripe tomato, peeled and cut into chunks. If I do not feel too lazy to wash the food processor afterward, I might purée the tuna with capers, cornichons, and unsalted butter, which I then spread on grilled bread. Or I may not have anything with it at all, eating it as an open sandwich with buttered bread. Buttered bread or, even better, a buttered English muffin toasted dark, is what I like to eat with sardines that still have their skins and bones. I do not buy feeble-tasting boneless, skinless sardines.

If I feel like being extravagant, I might have Sardinian *bottarga*, the pressed and dried roe of mullets netted on that island's western coast, preparing it as they do in Sardinia. After removing the roe's membrane, I slice it paper thin and sandwich it between two shards of buttered cracker bread. Even better would be to use Sardinia's own sheet-music bread, *carta musica*, which I have made myself at those infrequent times when I have had a lot of energy to burn. It is a huge amount of work, but I make a lot of it and it keeps for months. It is also available online, imported from Sardinia. Tuna *bottarga*, which comes from Sicily, is much sharper. After slicing it as thin as I can, I toss it with shredded Belgian endive, seasoning it with lemon juice and olive oil.

My husband calls me *mangia panini*, sandwich eater, because I will eat almost anything that is enclosed between two slices of bread. When I am in Italy, one of my favorite snacks is a sandwich Italians call *tost*. It is a grilled cheese sandwich whose ideal components are fontina cheese and cooked Parma ham. The cafés make it in a special toaster with a folding, vertical grill that lifts up and out. I make it for myself often because I find the combination of very crisp hot bread and superior melting cheese surpassingly comforting and fully satiating. It has to be carefully done with the right ingredients, otherwise it can turn out to be a stodgy piece of work.

I have thought about the apparent contradiction that someone who has dedicated most of her working life to cooking should be so reluctant, when she eats alone, to cook for herself. The explanation is that I consider cooking to be an act of love. I do enjoy the craft of cooking, of course, otherwise I would not have done so much of it, but that is a very small part of the pleasure it brings me. What I love is to cook for someone. To put a freshly made meal on the table, even if it is something very plain and simple, as long as it tastes good and is not a ready-to-heat something bought at the store, is a sincere expression of affection, it is an act of binding intimacy directed at whoever has a welcome place in your heart. And while other passions in your life may, at some point, begin to bank their fires, the shared happiness of good homemade food can last as long as we do.

Il Tost
(GRILLED CHEESE AND HAM SANDWICH,
ITALIAN STYLE)

YIELD: TWO *TOST*

Like many other Italian preparations, this appears to be so simple as to be almost banal. Banal is a bore, but simple can be sublime. To cross the line from the former to the latter you must be uncompromising about the ingredients. Packaged, sliced supermarket cheese won't do the trick. Nor will water-packed supermarket ham. Insist on flavorful imported cheese and sliced-to-order cooked ham, preferably Parma ham and preferably with some fat on it. Do it right and you may become as addicted to *tost* as most Italians are.

The bread used for *tost* in Italy is called *pane a cassetta*, which corresponds to very thin, sliced packaged white bread. I usually make it with Pepperidge Farm's Very Thin Sliced White, but I have also used the same brand's Very Thin Wheat, which I have grown fond of.

Four thin, square slices white bread

1½ tablespoons butter

2 ounces imported Italian Fontina cheese, or aged Swiss or Gruyère cheese sliced thin, or slivers of Parmigian-Reggiano cheese

Two slices cooked, unsmoked ham, preferably imported cooked Parma ham, but not prosciutto

A baking dish

1. Turn on the oven to 500° F.
2. Butter each slice of bread on one side only.

3. Cover the buttered side of each of two slices with cheese and top with one slice of ham.

4. Cover with the remaining slice of bread, buttered side facing in.

5. Place in the baking dish without overlapping.

6. Bake in the preheated oven for 5 minutes. If after 5 minutes the bread is not yet fully browned, bake for an additional minute.

7. Serve hot, cutting the *tost* diagonally in half if desired.

Making Soup in Buffalo

BEVERLY LOWRY

In the early 1960s I lived in Manhattan for five years, with a new husband, Glenn, who worked for the National Cotton Council, which was based in Memphis. The Cotton Council was staffed almost entirely with born Southerners who had more than happily moved away from home, north to the city. One of them, Charlotte Norman, had grown up and lived most of her life in southern Louisiana—Abbeville and then New Orleans—where food preparation was and is, of course, a very big deal. In her family, her father, called Boy, had been the cook; her mother, Thelma, was a school-teacher who did other things. After her husband died, Thelma had to ask where the oven broiler was.

Boy Norman traveled. But whenever he was at home, he and Charlotte and her sister Toni cooked the evening meal together. No shortcuts. They cooked by the standards set in their culture and their community, which were exceedingly high. Stirring the roux took as long as it took, and somebody had to stand over the pot stirring it until the flour-oil mix turned the proper grocery-sack brown. Usually, they didn't eat until nine or ten o'clock.

Charlotte lived alone in Manhattan, and it was she who taught me to respect and prepare food. I grew up in Mississippi. My mother, who was from Arkansas, had been a fairly adventurous cook herself—often making us curries and egg foo yong instead of the usual fried chicken and greens—but Charlotte's relationship to food went far beyond ingredients.

One Saturday afternoon when I went over to her apartment, I found her in her tiny kitchen, finishing up a Louisiana dish— might have been gumbo or étouffée, perhaps a batch of roux— and ladling it into small plastic containers for freezing.

Was she planning a dinner?

No, she said. They were for herself, so that when she came home from work she wouldn't have to start from scratch.

You cook for yourself? I asked. At twenty-two, I was more than a little sassy. I had never lived alone in my life.

Charlotte has this look, a straight-on gaze of exhausted befuddlement, the slightly scornful gaze of one who stands in wonderment at the other person's rank unknowing.

Why wouldn't I cook for myself? she said.

That was more than forty years ago. I can see her at that moment, as precisely today as if she said it last Saturday.

Charlotte and I cooked many, many meals together. Usually, nobody from the Cotton Council went back to the South for holidays. We couldn't afford the plane fare, or we just didn't want to go. During one Christmas season, Charlotte and I issued written invitations to a black-tie five-course meal in my apartment.

Using instructions from a *Gourmet* magazine, Charlotte boned a chicken, keeping the shape of the chicken intact so that the carver could slice straight through white meat and dark, breast to rump. On another occasion we made Diana Kennedy's mole de pollo, down to grinding spices and hot peppers in a *molcajete*. The preparation took all day and was not a success. We used the wrong kind of chocolate, didn't grind the peppers enough, drank too much tequila and missed a step—who knows? The dish was a flop. Exhausted by the time we got to the table, we dumped the chocolate chicken and went out to eat.

In time, once life has kicked us around a bit, sassiness cools. Since that Saturday in Charlotte's kitchen, I have lived in many places, sometimes alone, and have cooked many meals for myself, in small and large kitchens—some of them in furnished digs, outfitted with the cheapest, most basic kind of cookware. I would not say that I recall Charlotte's pointed question—which wasn't really a question—*every* time I cook and eat alone, but often as I sit quite happily alone at some table in some new town, I do.

Over the years I've settled on a few basic beliefs, one of which is that whatever we do for pleasure, we should try to do, or learn to do, and practice on occasion, in solitude. A kind of test to gauge our skills and see how deep the passion lies and to find out what it is we truly like, to discover—minus other tastes and preferences—what specifically gives us pleasure. We all have our eccentricities. Alone, we indulge.

And so, the solitary cook fixes her meal. She eats, enjoying what she's made however she likes, whether eating salad with her hands (as I like to do) or mopping up the last bit of sauce with bread or even—childlike—fingers. For many it's eating that is the hard part. What to look at or listen to. When to stop, how much to save.

So many details to attend to.

In my judgment, those who cook for themselves generally fall into two groups: the ones who, like Charlotte, prepare ahead and those who, like me, cook for the night, the moment, the one occasion. In the times I have lived alone and fed myself, I have routinely stuck to certain dishes, cooking them over and over again, until in memory, the place and the dish merge and become a single event. I never planned to do this—say, to fix only baked potatoes with a green of some kind, cooked or raw, in a particular kitchen in a certain town—but I could not seem to stop. Repetition became a ritual. When shopping for the night, I would stand in a market trying to convince myself to make something different tonight, not to buy the same one-third-pound slab of salmon, the same prewashed spinach, boned chicken breast, or plum tomatoes I bought the day before.

There was nothing I could do. The fact was, I *wanted* the same thing again and again. And so I yielded, bought the goods, took them home, cooked, and ate, accompanied usually by music, preferably a public radio station that played music I liked. And I am here to tell you, the pleasure never diminished. I was happy every time.

. . .

In the 1990s I lived in Missoula, Montana, for a few years. When I first went there, I was alone and lived in a very small furnished place, part of a big house near the university where I had a job as a visiting writer. The kitchen was probably the smallest I'd ever cooked in, and there was no dining room, just a table pushed against the wall, big enough for three if they weren't tall.

I was heavily into anchovies in those days. I fixed Guiliano Bugialli's pasta with tomatoes and anchovies, his orecchiete with anchovies and parsley, his whole cauliflower with anchovy sauce. On the burners, I blistered bell peppers to peel and eat with olive oil and anchovies, and sometimes prepared a dish of my own devising: roasted sliced eggplant and peppers, with anchovies, garlic, oregano, and olive oil. There was a very fine Italian market in Missoula, the Broadway Market, owned and run by Alfredo and Ann Cipolato. Cipolato—who often sang opera for us as we shopped—regularly stocked big cans of salt-packed anchovies, which I regularly purchased and used. I also bought wine and pasta there and probably drank a lot of the wine alone, because whenever I'm in Missoula I always drink a lot of wine and have a lot of fun.

Mornings in Missoula, I made coffee and watched out the window. On sunny days students walked to class in beach attire even though the temperature was still in the thirties. Before I went to teach my class, I worked on a novel, *The Track of Real Desires,* the entire plot of which is based around a dinner party. I finished a draft of the book there.

Alone, I fed my appetite for anchovies. And fed it. Never sated, never bored.

In Tuscaloosa, Alabama, some years later, on another visiting-writer gig, I was living alone while in residence with a man I'd been with for some time, an actor, who was British but had a green card. By then, each of us had disappeared into a life apart but we didn't know it yet and hadn't parted. He slept late; I got up early. I loved those hours and sometimes went down to the quite large, if woefully equipped, kitchen, and made myself a batch of whole-wheat banana or apple pancakes, from scratch, with maple syrup. How happy I was during those minutes alone, reading the newspaper, with the radio playing softly beside me. I would cook myself two pancakes and vow no more, then scrape the rest of the batter out and cook another. How I love maple syrup! When the actor went back to England to visit family and I was truly alone in Tuscaloosa, for supper I cooked eggs, usually a frittata, with whatever vegetables I had on hand. Or pancakes. Sometimes oatmeal.

Breakfast starts the day; maybe by eating breakfast food at all hours, I was hoping to affect a new one, I don't know. When my Alabama gig was finished, the actor returned to London and I went to Wimberley, Texas, and then Austin, where I lived alone for fifteen months.

Sometimes we find home, even for a temporary stay, and settle in. Old friends and family lived in Austin and I settled in there, in a boxlike little house not far from the university. Closer still was the magnificent Central Market, where I could choose

daily from at least eleven kinds of sweet peppers and thirteen va-
rieties of store-prepared sausage. In Austin I dabbled and experimented in the kitchen, but always came back to what I loved at
that time: high-protein smoothies in the morning, pasta at night.
It was about then that I began a fixation on salad, I think because by that time, you could buy it prewashed. At Central Market I could choose among many combinations: romaine, baby
romaine, red baby romaine, mesclun, baby spinach, radicchio
mix, mache mix . . . heaven.

I settled on penne rigate as my pasta of choice, usually
topped with a fresh plum tomato sauce and sometimes with
tuna or a combination of eggplant, peppers, and anchovies, as in
Missoula.

As for the smoothie, I was down on milk in those days, for no
other reason than temporary dislike and intolerance. This has
passed, but back then I stuck to apple juice and kept sliced
frozen bananas in the freezer for taste and froth, adding whatever other fruits were offered by Central Market, and a big
scoop of vanilla protein powder.

I had put my stuff in storage, and so in Austin I used borrowed furniture and kitchenware. Somebody gave me a cheap
microwave, something I'd never owned. I used it a lot, warming
up last night's pasta. I usually ate to one of the great KUT radio
shows, Paul Ray, Phil Music, or Larry Monroe.

I felt like they were there with me.

This is a tale about food, music, and love. By then, I was seeing another man. He showed up from time to time and after I
moved to D.C. from Austin, he was still in my life but making a
habit of not showing up anymore. When I ate alone I tried not

to think of him but it was hard. By then, I'd bought a George Foreman grill, which became my cooker of choice. I'd buy a slab of tuna or salmon or a boneless chicken breast, season it a little, then slam it between the plates. I called it "Georging," as in, I just Georged some salmon. I seasoned the tuna with garlic and rosemary; the salmon with ginger and garlic; the chicken breasts with a lemony mustard marinade. Salad, bread. WPFW played great jazz, Caribbean, reggae, rhythm and blues. I had a Sam's Club combination TV and VCR machine with a ten-inch screen. Sometimes I had raspberry sorbet and vanilla frozen yogurt for dessert.

Eating alone at home with music felt a lot less lonely than eating out in a café or at a bar.

My apartment in D.C. was in the trees. In the spring, when dogwoods bloomed, I felt like I was living in a snow world.

That summer I went to Marfa, Texas, for almost three months. There, in a former army barracks turned into an artists' colony, I finished a biography and dined on baked potatoes—sometimes russets, sometimes yams—either with spinach and red onions sautéed in olive oil (or spinach and garlic, or spinach, onions, and mushrooms), or a salad. I would open up the potato and add some olive oil, salt, and pepper, then dump the green stuff on top. It is hard to say how much this meal pleased me at this time.

I had borrowed a boombox from somebody but didn't have many CDs. Out there in the high desert the only radio station I could get was country music AM. I listened anyway. At night I did exercises to Moby and played Macy Gray's first album. Or, once the heat had dissipated a little, took a bike ride into the mountains, on a blacktop road that ended in Mexico.

Last year I lived in Fresno for four and a half months. By that time I was sharing my life with the man who had previously given me the runaround in D.C., and we were good together, but because of another visiting job, we were apart for that time. In Fresno, I depended on Trader Joe's for inspiration and meals. I had become hooked on a salad I used to get at Così in D.C., the one they called their signature salad: lettuce, pistachios, grapes, gorgonzola. I varied this in many ways, using pears or figs and walnuts, with feta or Roquefort. With the salad I ate The Trader's butternut squash soup, usually topped with some cumin, cilantro, and a dollop of plain yogurt. I couldn't get enough, and cleaned up the last drops from the bowl with T.J. whole-grain bread. I began to think of the store as run by a particular man, The Trader, the way people used to turn Betty Crocker into a real woman.

One time while shopping I told myself enough was enough and I bought The Trader's red pepper soup instead. It was good but not what I was looking for.

The next day I went back to butternut.

I drank wine from Trader Joe's, ate protein bars from Trader Joe's, drank The Trader's coffee, tea and the Italian fizzy water he sold in blue bottles.

Sometimes I went out and ate. When the World Series playoffs began and the Astros made the semifinals, I would go to a sports bar, where I ate food and watched the ball games.

Fresno had a great jazz station, KFSR. I'd bought a nice little Sony set with a remote control. It was in the living room next to my desk, down the hall from the bedroom. When I woke up I hit the remote, to hear David Aus or Joe Moore. At night, eating my soup, I listened to Mr. Leonard or Blues Mondays. I lived in an

apartment complex set up for transient businesspeople. Everything was furnished, including a dieffenbachia in the corner with a
tag on it reminding us to please dust the leaves. The pots and pans
were cheap and tissue thin. I rarely used them but relied instead
on the microwave that came standard in every apartment. One
time, however, I did make a pot of soup. One Wednesday, Mark
Bittman ran a recipe for Luccan farro soup in his *New York Times*
column. Having never heard of farro but always trusting Bittman,
I couldn't resist. I made a pot for myself and then (because there
was so much of it and under such conditions of transience I had
no intention of putting food by) took a big bowl over to share with
friends. They told me they feasted on it for a couple of days.

When the semester was over, I left central California but managed to hold on to that recipe. I have made the soup often; in
fact, I just made it last week. Still good. Still reminding me of
nights alone in Fresno.

I have also discovered a version of butternut squash soup
similar to Trader's, one with roasted apples and garlic added to
the puréed squash.

Charlotte has long since moved back to Louisiana. Her New
Orleans house is situated only yards from the 17th Street Canal
that overran so many neighborhoods after Hurricane Katrina.
But, miraculously, her house did not float away. Her floors and
appliances were ruined, and had to be replaced. Now she has a
kitchen again.

And I am living in Buffalo, New York, where I never thought
I would be. It's a good city. I make a lot of soup in Buffalo.

Que Será Sarito: An (Almost) Foolproof Plan to Never Ever Eat Alone Again

STEVE ALMOND

From time to time, a friend will drop by my place unannounced. Given that I am Jewish, I am required by Mosaic law to ask if they would like something to eat, and to ignore any utterances that fall short of *I thought you'd never ask*!

It is true that some visitors, after casting a glance around my kitchen—pausing, perhaps, to inspect the stalactites of gunk that have been known to beset the interior of my toaster oven—will issue a declination. But it is equally true that I can be persistent in this matter, as my good mother taught me.

More than a few brave souls have sighed and (sensing the inevitable) asked, "What did you have in mind?"

It is at this point that I strike a casual pose and respond, "I was thinking about a grill-curried shrimp quesarito with avocado raita."

To which they will respond, "A *what-what-what* with *what?*" allowing me the unrivaled pleasure of repeating myself, this time in italics: *"A grill-curried shrimp quesarito with avocado raita."* If you have not offered someone a Grill-Curried Shrimp Quesarito with Avocado Raita in an obnoxiously offhand manner, you are really only half alive.

Now: most of my friends are artists of some sort, meaning poor, hungry, aggrieved. They don't do a lot of parsing. My friend Kirk, for instance, has been known to finish a meal without (technically) inhaling, after which we often play a game called What Did Kirk Just Eat?

> Me: Okay, what did Kirk just eat?
> Kirk (after a thoughtful pause): Was it chicken?
> Me: No.
> Kirk: It had meat in it.

And so on. Every now and again, though, some actual working citizen sneaks past the tripwire and they generally want to know what I am feeding them, and how it got to be that color. I am offering this recipe for them, though before doing so I want to make a couple of observations regarding my motives in the kitchen realm.

It is certainly true that cooking is therapeutic, creative, and all those other faintly creepy self-helpish words. I would love to tell you that learning to cook was part of my journey toward actualization. I would love to tell Oprah this. I would love to tell Oprah this while weeping. But I learned to cook for a much simpler reason: in the abject hope that people would spend time with me if I put good things in their mouths. It is, in other words (like practically everything else I do), a function of my desperation for emotional connection and acclaim.

Most writers are driven by the same impolite needs, though it is terribly unfashionable to admit that this is the case. Ironically, the act of writing itself is a terribly inefficient way of gratifying these needs, particularly in this age of joyous illiteracy. Cooking makes a lot more sense.

I could have a jolly old time dating all this back to my lonely childhood, but let's not and say we did, because I've got a recipe to present, and because I also want to say a quick thing about what's come to be known as the foodie movement.

Here's what I want to say: while I absolutely love fine food and laud the quality of attention that goes into preparing and consuming same, I worry (quite a lot, actually) that there is something morally queasy about the arrangement. After eating a particularly fabulous meal, I often wonder whether the combined energy spent on the vittles—not just the time and money, but the imaginative passion—might not be better spent on a broader, altruistic effort.

Some of this is your standard Jewish guilt, a way of punishing myself for the unbearable pleasures of the palate. But it's also true that a certain share of the left-wing zeal in this country has turned away from the looming crises we face as a species, and toward ornate sensual gratifications.

This is a theory I have stolen, nearly verbatim, from my father, who has spent much of his adulthood considering such questions. Then again, he is also capable of preparing a chicken cacciatore that would make Colonel Sanders weep for several weeks straight, so I'm not sure where that leaves us.

My own recipes—fancy-schmancy names notwithstanding—tend to run against foodie doctrine. I'm into simple ingredients and simple preparation, by which I mean (of course) that I'm into impressing people without having to work terribly hard.

I'm also big on adaptability. A good recipe is not Church doctrine. It should allow for improvisation based on personal taste. Cooking as obedience bores me. So everything that follows should be taken with a grain of salt—and not the gourmet fleur de sel stuff, just plain salt.

To begin: buy yourself some raw tiger-tail shrimp, medium size, two pounds at least. Why tiger-tail? Because they are the coolest to order. Other customers will look at you and think, *Well, how do you like that? Tiger-tail shrimp. Here is a man who knows what he wants!*

I get the kind with the shell still on, because it is slightly cheaper and because I enjoy the act of shucking them, and most especially using the verb *shuck* in conversation. The classic example being "I'd love to escort you to the Oscars, Paris, but I've got a lot of shucking to do."

Marinate the suckers in teriyaki, brown sugar, and toasted sesame oil, and give them a healthy dusting of curry powder. Refrigerate for an hour while you get your coals going, and soak some wood chips. (Note: If you're going to go to the trouble of grilling, you are legally required to smoke.)

Shrimp cook *really fast* and they get all rubbery if you overgrill them, so you have to set them down quick and flip them *as soon as they start to pink*. You want a bite that's juicy and pliant. Do a test run of one if you're not sure. And remember that the shrimp continue to cook off the grill.

If you've done this right, the shrimp should have a nice yellow tint from the curry, and some brown around the edges where the sugar caramelized. Nice. Store all the shrimp in the same container. This is crucial because the shrimp are going to release smoky juices that are basically, by weight, more precious than flu vaccine.

Next, the lettuce. I generally go with finely chopped iceberg, because I like the crunch, and it's cheap and easy to locate. If you're feeling flush, you can try Boston lettuce, which has an earthier flavor.

Tomatoes. If you are buying from the store, there is absolutely no reason you should be using any tomato other than the roma. They have the best flavor, by far. Chop them fine.

As to the cheese . . . there are many people (such as my girlfriend) who favor what I call "death cheese." This, simply put, is any cheese that tastes like death. Or like the inside of someone's mouth who has been dead for several weeks. That is neither here nor there, really, but it's worth noting that if you're one of these folks who loves death cheese, you should be eating that stuff straight, not putting it in recipes that call for some modicum of balance. For the quesarito, I recommend Monterey Jack, a mild cheese that complements smoked meats.

The only basic left is the avocado raita. It is almost embarrassingly easy to make. Pit two ripe avocados and chop. Add your favorite guacamole mix (mine happens to be Concord, though I use only half the recommended dose). If you want to keep it all from scratch, ditch the mix and add four cloves of roasted garlic, salt, minced onions, and cayenne pepper to taste. Mix with half a cup of plain lowfat yogurt. Done.

Important: you should have all of these ingredients set out in cool little ceramic bowls, like on the cooking shows. This will make you feel incredibly competent and inspire in your guests an unreasonable sense of awe.

We are now ready for the tortilla. I use the burrito-style flour ones. They allow for a larger playing surface and are more supple than corn. Plunk one down on the skillet (or nonstick pan) and let one side get slightly browned. Now flip it and sprinkle cheese over the entire thing. Put a lid over the tortilla, as if you were cooking an egg sunny-side up. The reason you do this is to melt the cheese quicker. It is also one of those moves that make you look like a real pro.

Take the tortilla off the heat and scatter the shrimp. If you have done this right, the shrimp will stick to the melted cheese. Now slide the tortilla onto a plate with a subtle but discernible flourish. Slather on the avocado raita and layer the tomatoes and lettuce.

Now you are ready for your pièce de résistance: pick up the container of shrimp and drizzle some of the smoky liquid that has gathered at the bottom across the quesarito. Don't play to the balconies here, but don't undersell the moment, either. Remember: for the lonely, cooking is not just self-maintenance. It is a powerful form of sexual marketing.

By all rights, your guest should by this time be in a state of minor bedazzlement, despite the fact that you have done little more than the average Taco Bell worker. This is one of the beauties of Mexican cuisine: Nothing is julienned. Nothing is blanched. All you do is grate, chop, and plop. And yet the resulting meal *appears complex*. In fact, it is the humility of the cooking process that lends the use of gourmet ingredients this robust irony.

As to what to do next . . . that's a tricky question. Some people like to fold the quesarito and eat it like a taco. Others fold it like a burrito. Others just try to eat it as is, pizza style. I generally leave my guests to figure out what they want, though I strongly discourage the use of fork and knife. I do so not merely to embarrass them (though that can never be entirely discounted in my case) but because food should be directly addressed by the mouth, particularly if it has been freshly prepared for you.

That said, if you are cooking for a guest the emphasis should be on their desires, not your virtuosity. Having served this meal several thousand times over the years, I now customize my quesaritos. If someone wants a nice, crispy wallop of fat, I add some peanut oil to the pan and pan-fry the tortilla. Or you can throw respectability out the window (as I so incessantly do) and flick down a pat of butter. Likewise, if they want the decadent version of the raita, use sour cream rather than yogurt. For the digestively fearless, try mascarpone cheese.

And by no means are you limited to the ingredients I've set out. They are merely the baseline. Feel free to grill up some Vidalia onion or portabellos when the shrimp are done. Whatever.

I realize this sounds like a lot of hassle, but the trick here is that you're not preparing a single meal. All the ingredients cited above can and should be stored in your fridge. In the restaurant biz, this is known—somewhat ominously—as preassembly. All you have to do is pull out the Tupperware, pour the ingredients into those cool little bowls, and heat the tortilla with cheese. Total prep time: five minutes. You can make six of these suckers in half an hour.

This brings us to another important issue: marijuana use.

In short, I condone it.

Obviously, the quesarito is going to taste better if you go fresh every time out. But let's be realistic: as a writer, you only have so many hours each day, and most of them will be swallowed by procrastination and the ensuing guilt. Try to remember, also, that your friends (though you are duty bound to feed them) are ungrateful freeloaders.

Which leads me to my final point: the dangers of ulteriority in the creative process. As I've indicated, preparing food for someone else is a tremendous rush. The thing you created gets eaten right before your eyes. You are paid many fine compliments. You are asked admiring questions about your raita prowess. People burp heartily, at least in the Russian countryside.

Such overt forms of recognition are rare for writers. You are forced to work alone. Most of the bad prose out there is, in fact, the result of insecurity about anticipated audience reaction. Gaudy metaphors, wasteful adverbs, hollow emotional assertions, implausible plot twists—all arise from the same essential neurosis. And yet the less you worry about the reader, the freer you are to focus on the people who actually matter: your characters.

The same thing applies to cooking. The well-executed quesarito will certainly lure some company to the table. But in the best cases, we cook to honor the process and the ingredients, the human capacity for edible invention—and to make nourishing the delicious ache of solitude.

Which is my roundabout way of confessing that, while I may

prepare my quesaritos in the devout hope a friend will drop by, on most evenings a friend does not drop by, and I am left to eat alone. This depresses me. Eating alone depresses me. It makes me feel the terrible loneliness of the world, all those men on barstools, with their hungry eyes and eager stories, all those women languishing before the soaps. And it embarrasses me. It makes me feel like a failure: the needy guy who eats alone. The needy guy who went to all this trouble, made everything just so, and waits by the door in his special quesarito tux with matching quesarito cummerbund. And (of course): it makes me feel guilty. To lavish such tender energies on a meal *implies* that it be served to others. Did I learn nothing from my good mother, who spent so many years returning from work exhausted, only to prepare delicious meals for her grabby, ingrate sons—baked chicken and rice, meatloaf, enchiladas—always serving herself last, almost re-luctantly, scraping the sticky left-behinds onto her plate?

But okay, let's assume I get past all this. I still face a final, cold truth: eating alone isn't natural. Life's greatest sensual pleasure (or at least its most consistently attainable) should be shared. I hap-pen to believe that humans were born to feed one another. The meal is our celebration of nurturance, our secular communion.

Does this mean that I starve myself when I can't find com-pany? Not quite. What I do, though, is put off eating until I'm ravenous. I also deny myself the richest possibilities. I don't throw that pat of butter into the pan (though I wish to). I scrimp on the smoked shrimp. It's a little deal I make with myself, just in case someone shows up later. Then I sit down with my quesar-ito and a glass of sweet juice and, when I can bear the hunger no longer, I go to town.

Grill-Curried Shrimp Quesarito with Avocado Raita

SERVES 1

7 to 8 tiger-tail shrimp

¼ cup teriyaki sauce

2 tablespoons dark brown sugar

1 tablespoon toasted sesame oil

½ teaspoon curry powder (or to taste)

¼ cup yogurt

¼ cup guacamole (see recipe, page 123)

1 burrito-style flour tortilla

1 ounce Monterey Jack, shredded

½ roma tomato, diced

1 handful of iceberg lettuce, chopped

Soak the shrimp in a marinade of teriyaki, brown sugar, and toasted sesame oil, dust with curry powder, and smoke on the grill.

Combine yogurt and guacamole to create the raita.

Pan-fry the flour tortilla and layer with cheese.

Layer with shrimp, tomato, lettuce, and raita.

Eat, using mouth and hands in conjunction.

The Year of Spaghetti
A short story
HARUKI MURAKAMI

Nineteen seventy-one was the Year of Spaghetti.

In 1971 I cooked spaghetti to live, and lived to cook spaghetti. Steam rising from the aluminum pot was my pride and joy, tomato sauce bubbling up in the saucepan my one great hope in life.

I'd gone to a cooking specialty store and bought a kitchen timer and a huge aluminum cooking pot, big enough to bathe a German shepherd in, then went round all the supermarkets that catered to foreigners, gathering an assortment of odd-sounding spices. I picked up a pasta cookbook at the bookstore, and bought tomatoes by the dozen. I purchased every brand of spaghetti I could lay my hands on, simmered every kind of sauce known to man. Fine particles of garlic, onion, and olive oil swirled in the air, forming a harmonious cloud that penetrated every corner of my tiny apartment, permeating the floor and ceiling and walls, my clothes, my books, my records, my tennis racket, my bundles of old letters. It was a fragrance one might have smelled on ancient Roman aqueducts.

This is a story from the Year of Spaghetti, 1971 A.D.

As a rule I cooked spaghetti, and ate it, alone. I was convinced that spaghetti was a dish best enjoyed alone. I can't really explain why I felt that way, but there it is.

I always drank tea with my spaghetti and ate a simple lettuce-and-cucumber salad. I'd make sure I had plenty of both. I laid everything out neatly on the table, and enjoyed a leisurely meal, glancing at the paper as I ate. From Sunday to Saturday, one Spaghetti Day followed another. And each new Sunday started a brand-new Spaghetti Week.

Every time I sat down to a plate of spaghetti—especially on a rainy afternoon—I had the distinct feeling that somebody was about to knock on my door. The person who I imagined was about to visit me was different each time. Sometimes it was a stranger, sometimes someone I knew. Once, it was a girl with slim legs whom I'd dated in high school, and once it was myself, from a few years back, come to pay a visit. Another time, it was none other than William Holden, with Jennifer Jones on his arm.

William Holden?

Not one of these people, though, actually ventured into my apartment. They hovered just outside the door, without knocking, like fragments of memory, and then slipped away.

Spring, summer, and fall, I cooked away, as if cooking spaghetti were an act of revenge. Like a lonely, jilted girl throwing old love letters into the fireplace, I tossed one handful of spaghetti after another into the pot.

I'd gather up the trampled-down shadows of time, knead

them into the shape of a German shepherd, toss them into the roiling water, and sprinkle them with salt. Then I'd hover over the pot, oversized chopsticks in hand, until the timer dinged its plaintive tone.

Spaghetti strands are a crafty bunch, and I couldn't let them out of my sight. If I were to turn my back, they might well slip over the edge of the pot and vanish into the night. Like the tropical jungle waits to swallow up colorful butterflies into the eternity of time, the night lay in silence, hoping to waylay the prodigal strands.

Spaghetti alla parmigiana
Spaghetti alla napoletana
Spaghetti al cartoccio
Spaghetti aglio e olio
Spaghetti alla carbonara
Spaghetti della pina

And then there was the pitiful, nameless leftover spaghetti carelessly tossed into the fridge.

Born in heat, the strands of spaghetti washed down the river of 1971 and vanished.

And I mourn them all—all the spaghetti of the year 1971.

When the phone rang at three-twenty I was sprawled out on the tatami, staring at the ceiling. A pool of winter sunlight had formed in the place where I lay. Like a dead fly I lay there, vacant, in a December 1971 spotlight.

At first, I didn't recognize it as the phone ringing. It was more like an unfamiliar memory that had hesitantly slipped in between the layers of air. Finally, though, it began to take shape, and, in the end, a ringing phone was unmistakably what it was. It was one hundred percent a phone ring in one-hundred-percent real air. Still sprawled out, I reached over and picked up the receiver.

On the other end was a girl, a girl so indistinct that, by four-thirty, she might very well have disappeared altogether. She was the ex-girlfriend of a friend of mine. Something had brought them together, this guy and this indistinct girl, and something had led them to break up. I had, I admit, reluctantly played a role in getting them together in the first place.

"Sorry to bother you," she said, "but do you know where he is now?"

I looked at the phone, running my eyes along the length of the cord. The cord was, sure enough, attached to the phone. I managed a vague reply. There was something ominous in the girl's voice, and whatever trouble was brewing I knew I didn't want to get involved.

"Nobody will tell me where he is," she said in a chilly tone. "Everybody's pretending they don't know. But there's something important I have to tell him, so *please*—tell me where he is. I promise I won't drag you into this. Where is he?"

"I honestly don't know," I told her. "I haven't seen him in a long time." My voice didn't sound like my own. I was telling the truth about not having seen him for a long time, but not about the other part—I did know his address and phone number. Whenever I tell a lie, something weird happens to my voice.

No comment from her.

The phone was like a pillar of ice.

Then all the objects around me turned into pillars of ice, as if I were in a J. G. Ballard science fiction story.

"I really don't know," I repeated. "He went away a long time ago, without saying a word."

The girl laughed. "Give me a break. He's not that clever. We're talking about a guy who has to raise a noise no matter what he does."

She was right. The guy really was a bit of a dim bulb.

But I wasn't about to tell her where he was. Do that, and next I'd have *him* on the phone, giving me an earful. I was through with getting caught up in other people's messes. I'd already dug a hole in the backyard and buried everything that needed to be buried in it. Nobody could ever dig it up again.

"I'm sorry," I said.

"You don't like me, do you?" she suddenly said.

I had no idea what to say. I didn't particularly dislike her. I had no real impression of her at all. And it's hard to have a bad impression of somebody you have no impression of.

"I'm sorry," I said again. "But I'm cooking spaghetti right now."

"What?"

"I said I'm cooking spaghetti," I lied. I had no idea why I said that. But that lie was already a part of me—so much so that, at that moment at least, it didn't feel like a lie at all.

I went ahead and filled an imaginary pot with water, lit an imaginary stove with an imaginary match.

"So?" she asked.

I sprinkled imaginary salt into the boiling water, gently lowered a handful of imaginary spaghetti into the imaginary pot, set the imaginary kitchen timer for twelve minutes.

"So I can't talk. The spaghetti will be ruined."

She didn't say anything.

"I'm really sorry, but cooking spaghetti's a delicate operation."

The girl was silent. The phone in my hand began to freeze again.

"So could you call me back?" I added hurriedly.

"Because you're in the middle of making spaghetti?" she asked.

"Yeah."

"Are you making it for someone or are you going to eat it alone?"

"I'll eat it by myself," I said.

She held her breath for a long time, then slowly breathed out. "There's no way you could know this, but I'm really in trouble. I don't know what to do."

"I'm sorry I can't help you," I said.

"There's some money involved, too."

"I see."

"He owes me money," she said. "I lent him some money. I shouldn't have, but I had to."

I was quiet for a minute, my thoughts drifting toward spaghetti. "I'm sorry," I said. "But I've got the spaghetti going, so . . ."

She gave a listless laugh. "Goodbye," she said. "Say hi to your spaghetti for me. I hope it turns out OK."

"Bye," I said.

When I hung up the phone, the circle of light on the floor

had shifted an inch or two. I lay down again in that pool of light and resumed staring at the ceiling.

Thinking about spaghetti that boils eternally but is never done is a sad, sad thing.

Now I regret, a little, that I didn't tell the girl anything. Perhaps I should have. I mean, her ex-boyfriend wasn't much to start with—an empty shell of a guy with artistic pretensions, a great talker whom nobody trusted. She sounded as if she really were strapped for money, and, no matter what the situation, you've got to pay back what you borrow.

Sometimes I wonder what happened to the girl—the thought usually pops into my mind when I'm facing a steaming-hot plate of spaghetti. After she hung up, did she disappear forever, sucked into the four-thirty shadows? Was I partly to blame?

I want you to understand my position, though. At the time, I didn't want to get involved with anyone. That's why I kept on cooking spaghetti, all by myself. In that huge pot, big enough to hold a German shepherd.

Durum semolina, golden wheat wafting in Italian fields.

Can you imagine how astonished the Italians would be if they knew that what they were exporting in 1971 was really *loneliness?*

—*Translated by Philip Gabriel*

Out to Lunch

COLIN HARRISON

For the better part of two decades I have lunched alone in Manhattan restaurants several times each week. Although my work requires me to break bread with a continuous stream of fascinating (and self-fascinated) personalities, I still prefer, if given the choice, to eat by myself. It's not that I fancy my own company so much as I enjoy the company of complete strangers. I like the communal anonymity of watching people as they go about their lives, and a restaurant is a good place to do this. The best table in any restaurant, so far as I'm concerned, is in a corner next to a window. From that spot I can be entertained by the infinite variety of the street or the enclosed drama of the restaurant itself. There's *always* a lot to see.

I was introduced to the pleasures of eating alone at the VG Bar/Restaurant at the northwest corner of Broadway and Bleecker in the late 1980s, where the enormous plate-glass windows were so close to the sidewalk that I felt as if I had my own box seat on the live theater that was the city. Across the street and down a few steps from my office, the VG was a simple place, stripped down to the bare brick, with narrow aisles of wobbly tables and wooden ladder-back chairs. It helped that I was—and remain—not fussy about what I eat. With a burger or a tuna melt steaming on a plate in front of me, I happily watched three-card monte games, fire engines racing down Broadway, homeless people shuffling toward their doom, minor car accidents at the light, an infinity of leggy young models on their way to photo shoots in the neighborhood, loud packs of teenagers up to no good whatsoever, the occasional duo of fat-necked mob bill collectors calling on the businesses where payment was late, and the hunched widows of NYU professors who lived in the neighborhood and in winter appeared outside for a few hours of sunlight in the midday warmth.

I ate at the VG in every month, in every kind of weather. Rain, especially the kind of slashing cold rain that hits New York City in late fall, improved the voyeuristic fishbowl effect. Here I was, warm and dry, but a few inches beyond my nose, nature flung itself downward, blowing umbrellas inside out as the taxis sprayed puddles onto the sidewalk. And during several of the huge blizzards that hit the city in those years, I made my way through the falling, piled snow, eyeglasses wet with it, and watched as the traffic slushed its way slowly along, the cornices and pediments of the building façades piled with white. You could hear the wind howl as it tried to turn the corner at Broadway, and the plate-glass windows would be cold to the touch. The VG had a very moist German chocolate cake that was particularly delicious to eat when the weather outside was foul. Don't ask me why, it just was.

Turning my eyes toward the inside of the VG, which allowed

smoking back then, an atmospheric element I enjoyed, I could see the midday alcoholics already at the bar, the young waitresses clawing out a living in the city, having just arrived from Seattle or Denver or Des Moines in hopes of discovering the version of themselves that they'd always dreamed about. The waitresses cycled through quickly, the very pretty ones finding better jobs or rich boyfriends within days of arriving, and the less beguiling settling in for a few months, or more. The most permanent employees were the Mexican busboys and cooks, although the VG had a couple of bartenders who had earned their stripes. The bar, a long, beautiful curved piece of mahogany, had been salvaged from some greater origin—a swanky hotel or midtown restaurant, or even an ocean liner, for all I knew—and on the wall next to its last seat hung a Nynex pay phone; here, while leaning back against the wall, it was possible to simultaneously knock back a beer, smoke, and make a phone call. The staff paid no attention to the wall soiled by heads and hands, nor to the tiny phone numbers etched in pencil and pen around the phone. The proximity of alcohol to the telephone attracted a stream of marginal middle-aged men whose loud conversations announced their identities as struggling salesmen working lower Manhattan territories or gambling addicts calling in their afternoon racetrack or baseball bets, as well as an endless cast of struggling writers, painters, musicians, photographers, composers, playwrights, sculptors, and would-be movie directors working some desperate angle that might forestall the inevitable.

When the dollar was cheap, the restaurant was flooded with German or Japanese tourists who irritated the regulars with their fat shopping bags. After lunch, the heat and smoke and chatter of the VG virtually expelled me out into the street, caffeinated and sugared up, ready to return to work. And yet the place *was* addictive, and once I found out that the restaurant quieted down after lunch, I began to stay there and work next to the window for longer stretches of time, leaving word at my office where I could be found, if truly necessary. Of course, I did not want to be found, and in those days before cell phones, rarely was.

The VG is gone now, replaced by a succession of increasingly upscale dining establishments and I, too, have moved on, through a series of restaurants where I came to know the menu, the staff, and the clientele. For a little while I frequented Fanelli's, an old establishment half a dozen blocks away, where the lunchers were older and more grizzled than those at the VG. I liked the patterned tin ceiling, the cup of chili, the old wood floor. The waitresses were pros—tough Manhattan chicks in their thirties and forties who had heard, seen, smoked, or ingested it all long ago. They seemed to like the guys in jean jackets with dirty hands—men who worked, not fops or frauds or delicate geniuses. But as SoHo boomed, Fanelli's became difficult to get into. Its authenticity made it a cool place, and the guys in jean jackets went elsewhere, as did I.

For a time in the early nineties, I ate in the Noho Star, another corner restaurant one long block to the east of the VG. Once while dining alone, I looked up from my plate of shrimp linguini to witness ten New York City police officers run south on Lafayette. They sprinted with great urgency, their guns drawn and pointing down. They passed by the window in less than five seconds, and I turned back to see if any of the restaurant's other patrons had noticed; they had not. In that same restaurant I spied over the years, and spied upon, John F. Kennedy, Jr., Sam Shepard, Gregory Hines, Wallace Shawn, and Lauren Hutton, among others. Dining alone, I noticed them all.

Now I work in midtown Manhattan. A few years ago, I found myself frequenting a not particularly distinguished Indian restaurant that I nonetheless returned to nearly every day. Within a week or two of my first visit the Indian waiters had pegged me as that rarest of patrons—the daily diner who never changes his order. I was an odd duck and that endeared me to them. Indeed, my familiarity with the restaurant and the staff became so complete that I was allowed to walk past parties of businesspeople waiting to be seated and proceed directly to what I came to think of as "my table," a two-seater next to a giant carved marble Ganesh. I was even allowed to enter and exit through what was more or less an unmarked doorway. The act of ordering became nothing more than a quick nod at whichever waiter glanced at me first. In this way, a plate of food usually arrived at my place within a minute or two of my arrival. One of the waiters, who often pumped me for possible connections in the hotel supply industry, despite my protestations that I had none, made it his special duty to brew a particular version of Indian tea for me. It was not as good as I pretended it was, but he meant well, and I didn't want to hurt his feelings.

Although the midtown crowds are not nearly as interesting to watch as the downtown crowds, I was content in this restaurant. The food was hot and fast, and no one much cared if I dropped a pea or spilled a little curry sauce on the white tablecloth. Again,

I began to work through and past lunch there, and it became known that if I could not be found in the office, chances were good that I was in the Indian restaurant nibbling on aloo matar gobhi amid the sitar music. I expected to eat there for the indefinite future, but not long ago one of the waiters in a black-and-white uniform came up to me during lunch and solemnly whispered that the restaurant would be closing the next day, due to a lack of patronage. He seemed anxious to break the news to me gently, perhaps worried that as I was a man of habits I might be undone by the forced change in my routine. I thanked him for the information and returned to the restaurant the next day, hours before it was to close. What was going to become of the place? I asked. It was being turned into an expensive steakhouse, I was told.

So it was, within a few months. Hoping to renew my affinity, I passed through the doors again and ate a good if expensive meal. The decor had been upgraded to a kind of forced luxuriousness. Not my thing. And the finely dressed waiters struck me as too hawkishly watchful; this was a place where you didn't drop a pea on the floor. I left the restaurant knowing I wouldn't return. The place itself had lost the casual indifference, the sloppy humanity, that had invited me to eat there every day.

Soon I was launched on my quest to find my next regular restaurant. I flirted with a two-story place festooned with shamrocks on the outside that I called "the Irish dump," having developed a fondness for their tuna melt, but the joint had too many televisions on, placed inescapably in every corner. From there I visited a kosher place a few doors down, which had a great view of the street from the second-floor window, and the added attraction of Diamond District jewelry dealers coming in to eat clannishly together. Little did the restaurant owners know that I was auditioning them for a regular place in my life. But although the food was criminally inexpensive and served by kindly Israeli matrons who seemed genuinely interested in whether I liked what they set down before me, I found the kosher dishes to be impossibly bland, overcooked into a sad paste. It's infrequent that I won't like a meal, as long as it's *hot,* but this stuff was— well, not great. So I moved on, somewhat disconsolately, through several of the panini and pizza joints on Forty-eighth Street, experimenting with yet another Indian restaurant a block west, also a second-floor joint where you climb a narrow, irregular stairwell. But this didn't do it; neither did a cheap sushi place with a great window seat. I quite enjoy the well-known Café Un Deux Trois a few blocks to the south, which has elegant food, great windows, and a fantastic people scene inside, but it's pricey if you're going to eat there every day. And maybe a little too visible.

No, I'm looking for a joint. My version of the VG ten years later. The right combination of street view, grease, and ambience. A great place that doesn't take itself too seriously. Not too expensive, either. With a decent burger, perhaps. It's clear I'll have to keep looking. Just last week I extended my search down Fifth Avenue, not discovering any place I liked. I'll find it, though. My new lunch place has got to be around here somewhere, and when I see it, I'll know.

Dining Alone

MARY CANTWELL

A gray and muggy afternoon. The walker returning from an errand that was as dreary as the day is crossing a street near Times Square. Behind her two teenage hookers are standing in a doorway; ahead there's a man selling funny hats. Beyond him is the man who sells incense, and beyond him the one who sells fake Vuitton bags. Beyond both a bag lady is perched on her usual branch, a fire hydrant, gumming something out of a cardboard carton.

The walker turns into a Japanese restaurant, sits at the counter, and orders *sushi* and Scotch on the rocks. Halfway through the Scotch and the third *tekkamaki* she suddenly realizes that she is happy. But it's not the food and drink alone that have lifted her spirits. It's watching the *sushi* chef wielding his knives and the customers wielding their chopsticks. It's picking up the threads of conversations, imagining the speakers' lives, and following laughter as it rises to the ceiling. The walker is, of course, myself, and when I leave that crowded, noisy room for that sad street I have been fed in more ways than are known to cooks.

There are people who bring books to restaurants, and who hide behind them, blind and deaf to everything beyond their pages. They hide behind menus, too, and order carelessly, and they never glance at the other diners. Maybe they're afraid the glance will reveal a hunger that has nothing to do with food. Or maybe they are so ashamed of being companionless that they court invisibility. But I am not one of them, because to me a restaurant is a theater, and my table a seat on the aisle.

The first time I ever dined alone—dined, that is, in a restaurant that had tablecloths, waiters, and large, stiff menus—was in London many years ago. I had gone there ahead of my husband for a few days of bookstores and museums, and I had not imagined that I would be lonely. But I was, and I saw the city with the eyes of someone who was peering through smoke. I lived on Wimpeys and Wipseys—pathetic versions of American burgers and shakes—at a nearby Lyons', and I went to bed early, believing that sleep would shorten the days until he arrived. But each night I woke around two o'clock, to stare at the ceiling and the thin line of light from the hallway under the door and the white curtains stirring in the sullen September air.

Early on the third evening, however, I passed a restaurant at which my husband and I had eaten on a previous trip. It was in Leicester Square and famous for its fish; I thought of Scottish salmon and Dover sole and, without thinking any further, walked right in.

The headwaiter was startled. I was young, I was alone, and besides the hour was ridiculous. Perhaps he thought I was there to see whom I could pick up, or perhaps he was simply trying to spare me the embarrassment I was bound to feel when I saw that ladies did not dine alone in so fashionable a place. In any case he put me in the back, by the kitchen door, and I, not realizing the insult, settled in happily and unfolded my napkin.

The salmon was as good as I thought it would be, and so was the sole, and I drank a white wine I remembered my husband once ordering. The restaurant filled with men who looked like Trevor Howard and women who looked like Celia Johnson, and I eavesdropped on two middle-aged couples discussing the Queen. "She likes hock, you know," one wife said while the others marveled, and I, citizen of a country in which a president's taste for bourbon, say, is interesting only if it drowns him, marveled too.

Outside, moviegoers were lining up for the old-fashioned picture palaces in Leicester Square, and buskers were assembling with their flaming torches and their golden balls and their tap shoes. And I, because I was eating the food of this particular country, listening to its dialogue, and spying on its entertainment, was part of its spin round the sun.

When I refused coffee the waiter, thinking it might be beyond my purse, leaned down and whispered, "It's all right. It comes with the meal." "No thank you," I said, "I don't like coffee," and paid the bill with a flourish. Then I sailed, rather than walked, out and if I had left a wake I wouldn't be surprised. Pleasure had transformed me from a leaking skiff into a three-masted schooner, and I was running before the wind.

When my husband finally got to London I was glad to see him, but I have never thought of that first evening I dined (in the grand sense of the word) alone as an evening I spent without him. Rather I think of it as the first I ever really spent with myself. We—that other person with whom one's conversation is perpetual and I—were free to concentrate on everything that was assaulting our senses, which is why the sensations are remembered so clearly now.

Since then I've dined alone a lot because I've traveled a lot and wouldn't think of incarcerating myself in a hotel room, captive to room service and fears I've read about but do not understand. Why should it take courage, as I'm told it sometimes does, to treat oneself as generously as one would a guest?

It wasn't courage, for instance, but a terrible hunger for lobster mayonnaise that once drove me to dinner in the garden of a restaurant in Dubrovnik. It was a romantic garden, I suppose, with rosebushes and leafy walls and candles on every table, and I was the only person there who was dining alone. But an old woman sitting in the second-storey window of the building that backed the garden watched my every move. When the light failed—it was summer and the sun set very late—and a younger woman came and took her away, I waved at her with that dippy bend of the fingers one gives to babies. I was saying good-bye because we had, in a sense, dined together.

Nor was it courage but an enthusiasm for the faintly seedy that took me to the dining room of a hotel in Istanbul. The hotel was respectable but run-down and past its prime, and the man who played old show tunes was as dusty as the potted palms that drooped over his piano. I, who might have been created by Mary McCarthy, stared at characters out of Graham Greene and wondered at our unlikely conjunction. Meanwhile the pianist played songs from *South Pacific*.

There was a time, though, when I did need a bit of courage: when all I had to wear for dinner in a rather fancy place in Ankara was a sweater and corduroy pants tucked into lace-up boots. But I stood very straight when I asked for the table, and there was no pause before I got it. Good posture, it seems, will take you far if what you have to navigate is other people's notions of propriety.

Nonetheless there is a restaurant to which I will never be brave enough to go by myself. It is close to the house in which I grew up, and its menu hasn't varied since it opened, which must have been when my parents were newlyweds. Its specialties are boiled live lobster and shoestring potatoes, the kind of coleslaw that isn't creamy, and a lemon meringue pie made by a woman who must be about 115 years old by now. I had my first mixed drink at that restaurant, a Martini, and drank it with what my father called policemen's sandwiches—oyster crackers split with one's thumbnail, heaped with horseradish, and closed again.

The restaurant is on a harbor and faces west, so my family and I try to get there in time for sunset. "Remember my daughter?" my mother is apt to say to any of her old friends who might be there. "She's all grown up now." Oh, how I am, with grown children of my own, but to her I am, as I suppose my daughters will be to me, a just-hatched butterfly still waiting for my wings to dry. This is no place for solitary dining. I couldn't see my fellow eaters for the memories.

But there is another place only a few miles away that belongs exclusively to me. It's on a raggedy waterfront street of spruced-up

houses and tumble-down derelicts, of secondhand shops and as-
piring *antiquaries,* and if the wind is right—or, more accurately,
wrong—the smell of fish from the packing plant down the road
can set one to staggering. I like that street; I walk it every weekend I am home to see if any of the shopkeepers are stupid
enough to sell a treasure for a song (they aren't) and to peek into
the windows of the latest restoration. Then I go to the restaurant, with its small patio and smaller bar, for fish chowder and a
view of the town's businessmen, the occasional secretarial pool
celebrating somebody's birthday, and those tweed-and-walking-
shoes widows who march through New England ever on the alert
for a new knitting yarn, a new decoration for the Christmas tree,
and the ultimate Indian pudding.

Two hundred miles due south is its city counterpart, also
on a raggedy street not far from the water. It's a new restaurant
with a silly name and two small rooms. The first has a bar to the
right and an elegantly programmed juxebox to the left. The second has small tables over which hang little stained-glass lamps
and on which stand mustard pots filled with daisies. The waiters
try hard to memorize the specials, the chef appears to be a
serious striver, and the neighbors have taken to dropping by.
So far I have been there only with friends but soon, I know,
there'll be a night when I find myself deserving a kindness.
When it comes, I'll take myself out for the calf's liver with
Sherry vinegar, a glass of the house red, and a look at how life is
being lived in one small restaurant on one small street in Greenwich Village on one night in 1985. And when I leave I'll be going
home happy.

A Is for Dining Alone
M. F. K. FISHER

... **a**nd so am I, if a choice must be made between most people I know and myself. This misanthropic attitude is one I am not proud of, but it is firmly there, based on my increasing conviction that sharing food with another human being is an intimate act that should not be indulged in lightly.

There are few people alive with whom I care to pray, sleep, dance, sing, or share my bread and wine. Of course there are times when this latter cannot be avoided if we are to exist socially, but it is endurable only because it need not be the only fashion of self-nourishment.

There is always the cheering prospect of a quiet or giddy or warmly somber or lightly notable meal with "One," as Elizabeth Robins Pennell refers to him or her in *The Feasts of Autolycus*. "*One* sits at your side feasting in silent sympathy," this lady wrote at the end of the last century in her mannered and delightful book. She was, at this point, thinking of eating an orange[1] in southern Europe, but any kind of food will do, in any clime, so long as *One* is there.

I myself have been blessed among women in this respect—which is of course the main reason that, if *One* is not there, dining alone is generally preferable to any other way for me.

Naturally there have been times when my self-made solitude has irked me. I have often eaten an egg and drunk a glass of jug-wine, surrounded deliberately with the trappings of busyness, in a hollow Hollywood flat near the studio where I was called a writer, and not been able to stifle my longing to be anywhere but

---

1. Probably the best way to eat an orange is to pick it dead-ripe from the tree, bite into it once to start the peeling, and after peeling eat a section at a time.

Some children like to stick a hollow pencil of sugarcandy through a little hole into the heart of an orange and suck at it. I never did.

Under the high-glassed Galeria Vittorio Emanuele in Milan before the bombs fell, the headwaiters of the two fine restaurants would peel an orange at your table with breath-taking skill and speed, slice it thin enough to see through, and serve it to you doused to your own taste with powdered sugar and any of a hundred liquors.

In this country Ambrosia is a dessert as traditionally and irrefutably Southern as pecan pie. My mother used to tell me how fresh and good it tasted, and how pretty it was, when she went to school in Virginia, a refugee from Iowa's dearth of proper *fin de siècle* finishing schools. I always thought of it as old-fashioned, as something probably unheard of by today's bourbons. I discovered only lately that an easy way to raise an un-ladylike babble of protest is to say as much in a group of Confederate Daughters—and here is the proof, straight from one of their mouths, that their local gods still sup on

Ambrosia

    6 fine oranges
    1½ cups grated coconut, preferably fresh
    1½ cups sugar
    Good sherry

Divide peeled oranges carefully into sections, or slice thin, and arrange in layers in a glass bowl, sprinkling each layer generously with sugar and coconut. When the bowl is full, pour a wine glass or so of sherry over the layers and chill well.

there, in the company of any of a dozen predatory or ambitious or even kind people who had *not* invited me.

That was the trouble: nobody did.

I cannot pretend, even on an invisible black couch of daydreams, that I have ever been hounded by Sunset Boulevardiers who wanted to woo me with caviar and win me with Pol Roger; but in my few desolate periods of being without *One* I have known two or three avuncular gentlemen with a latent gleam in their eyes who understood how to order a good mixed grill with watercress. But, for the most part, to the lasting shame of my female vanity, they have shied away from any suggestion that we might dally, gastronomically speaking. "Wouldn't dare ask *you*," they have murmured, shifting their gaze with no apparent difficulty or regret to some much younger and prettier woman who had never read a recipe in her life, much less written one, and who was for that very reason far better fed than I.

It has for too long been the same with the ambitious eaters, the amateur chefs and the self-styled gourmets, the leading lights of food-and-wine societies. When we meet, in other people's houses or in restaurants, they tell me a few sacrosanct and impressive details of how they baste grouse with truffle juice, then murmur, "Wouldn't dare serve it to *you*, of course," and forthwith invite some visiting potentate from Nebraska, who never saw a truffle in his life, to register the proper awe in return for a Lucullan and perhaps delicious meal.[2]

---

2. Crêpes, approximately Suzette, are the amateur gourmet's delight, and more elaborately sogged pancakes have been paddled about in more horrendous combinations of butter, fruit juices, and ill-assorted liqueurs in the name of gastronomy than it is well to think on.

And the kind people—they are the ones who have made me feel the loneliest. Wherever I have lived, they have indeed been kind—up to a certain point. They have poured cocktails for me, and praised me generously for things I have written to their liking, and showed me their children. And I have seen the discreetly drawn curtains to their family dining rooms, so different from the uncluttered, spinsterish emptiness of my own one room. Behind the far door to the kitchen I have sensed, with the mystic materialism of a hungry woman, the presence of honest-to-God fried chops, peas and carrots, a jello salad,[3] and lemon

---

A good solution to this urge to stand up at the end of a meal and flourish forks over a specially constructed chafing dish is to introduce local Amphytrions to some such simple elegance as the following, a recipe that was handed out free, fifteen years ago in France, by the company that made Grand Marnier:

Dissolve 3 lumps of sugar in 1 teaspoon of water. Add the zest of an orange, sweet butter the size of a walnut, and a liqueur glass of Grand Marnier. Heat quickly, pour over hot, rolled crêpes, set aflame, and serve.

3. The following dish has almost the same simplicity as the preceding ones, but where they are excellent, this is, to my mind, purely horrible.

It is based on a packaged gelatin mixture which is almost a staple food in America. To be at its worst, which is easy, this should be pink, with imitation and also packaged whipped milk on top. To maintain this gastronomical level, it should be served in "salad" form, a small quivering slab upon a wilted lettuce leaf, with some such boiled dressing as the one made from the rule my maternal grandmother handed down to me, written in her elegantly spiderish script.

I can think of no pressure strong enough to force me to disclose, professionally, her horrid and austere receipt. Suffice it to say that it succeeds in producing, infallibly, a kind of sour, pale custard, blandly heightened by stingy pinches of mustard and salt, and made palatable to the most senile tongues by large amounts of sugar and flour and good water. Grandmother had little truck with foreign luxuries like olive oil, and while she thought nothing of having the cook make a twelve-egg cake every Saturday, she could not bring herself to use more than the required one egg in any such frippery as a salad dressing. The truth probably is that salads themselves were suspect in her culinary pattern, a grudging concession to the Modern Age.

meringue pie—none of which I like and all of which I admire in theory and would give my eyeteeth to be offered. But the kind people always murmur, "We'd love to have you stay to supper sometime. We wouldn't *dare*, of course, the simple way we eat and all."

As I leave, by myself, two nice plump kind neighbors come in. They say howdo, and then good-by with obvious relief, after a polite, respectful mention of culinary literature as represented, no matter how doubtfully, by me. They sniff the fine creeping straightforward smells in the hall and living room, with silent thanks that they are not condemned to my daily fare of quails financière, pâtè de Strasbourg truffé en brioche, sole Marguéry, bombe vanille au Cointreau. They close the door on me.

I drive home by way of the corner Thriftimart to pick up another box of Ry Krisp, which with a can of tomato soup and a glass of California sherry will make a good nourishing meal for me as I sit on my tuffet in a circle of proofs and pocket detective stories.

It took me several years of such periods of being alone to learn how to care for myself, at least at table. I came to believe that since nobody else dared feed me as I wished to be fed, I must do it myself, and with as much aplomb as I could muster. Enough of hit-or-miss suppers of tinned soup and boxed biscuits and an occasional egg just because I had failed once more to rate an invitation!

I resolved to establish myself as a well-behaved female at one or two good restaurants, where I could dine alone at a pleasant table with adequate attentions rather than be pushed into a corner and given a raw or overweary waiter. To my credit, I managed to carry out this resolution, at least to the point where two head-waiters accepted me: they knew I tipped well, they knew I wanted simple but exellent menus, and, above all, they knew that I could order and drink, all by myself, an apéritif and a small bottle of wine or a mug of ale, without turning into a maudlin, potential pick-up for the Gentlemen at the Bar.

Once or twice a week I would go to one of these restaurants and with carefully disguised self-consciousness would order my meal, taking heed to have things that would nourish me thoroughly as well as agreeably, to make up for the nights ahead when soup and crackers would be my fare. I met some interesting waiters: I continue to agree with a modern Mrs. Malaprop who said, "They are *so* much nicer than people!"

My expensive little dinners, however, became, in spite of my good intentions, no more than a routine prescription for existence. I had long believed that, once having bowed to the inevitability of the dictum that we must eat to live, we should ignore it and live to eat, in proportion of course. And there I was, spending more money than I should, on a grim plan which became increasingly complicated. In spite of the loyalty of my waiter friends, wolves in a dozen different kinds of sheep's clothing—from the normally lecherous to the Lesbian—sniffed at the high wall of my isolation. I changed seats, then tables. I read—I read everything from *Tropic of Cancer* to *Riders of the Purple Sage*. Finally I began to look around the room and hum.

That was when I decided that my own walk-up flat, my own script-cluttered room with the let-down bed, was the place for me. "Never be daunted in public" was an early Hemingway phrase that had more than once bolstered me in my timid twenties. I changed it resolutely to "Never be daunted in private."

I rearranged my schedule, so that I could market on my way to the studio each morning. The more perishable tidbits I hid in the watercooler just outside my office, instead of dashing to an all-night grocery for tins of this and that at the end of a long day. I bought things that would adapt themselves artfully to an electric chafing dish: cans of shad roe (a good solitary dish, since I always feel that nobody really likes it but me), consommé double, and such. I grew deliberately fastidious about eggs and butter; the biggest, brownest eggs were none too good, nor could any butter be too clover-fresh and sweet. I laid in a case or two of "unpretentious but delightful little wines." I was determined about the whole thing, which in itself is a great drawback emotionally. But I knew no alternative.

I ate very well indeed. I liked it too—at least more than I had liked my former can-openings or my elaborate preparations for dining out. I treated myself fairly dispassionately as a marketable thing, at least from ten to six daily, in a Hollywood studio story department, and I fed myself to maintain top efficiency. I recognized the dull facts that certain foods affected me this way, others that way. I tried to apply what I knew of proteins and so forth to my own chemical pattern, and I deliberately scrambled two eggs in a little sweet butter when quite often I would have liked a glass of sherry and a hot bath and to hell with food.

I almost never ate meat, mainly because I did not miss it and secondarily because it was inconvenient to cook on a little grill and to cut upon a plate balanced on my knee. Also, it made the one-room apartment smell. I invented a great many different salads, of fresh lettuces and herbs and vegetables, of marinated tinned vegetables, now and then of crabmeat and the like. I learned a few tricks to play on canned soups, and Escoffier as well as the Chinese would be astonished at what I did with beef bouillon and a handful of watercress or a teaspoonful of soy.

I always ate slowly, from a big tray set with a mixture of Woolworth and Spode; and I soothed my spirits beforehand with a glass of sherry or vermouth, subscribing to the ancient truth that only a relaxed throat can make a swallow. More often than not I drank a glass or two of light wine with the hot food: a big bowl of soup, with a fine pear and some Teleme Jack cheese; or two very round eggs, from a misnamed "poacher," on sourdough toast with browned butter poured over and a celery heart alongside for something crisp; or a can of bean sprouts, tossed with sweet butter and some soy and lemon juice, and a big glass of milk.

Things tasted good, and it was a relief to be away from my job and from the curious disbelieving impertinence of the people in restaurants. I still wished, in what was almost a theoretical way, that I was not cut off from the world's trenchermen by what I had written for and about them. But, and there was no cavil here, I felt firmly then, as I do this very minute, that snug misanthropic solitude is better than hit-or-miss congeniality. If *One* could not be with me, "feasting in silent sympathy," then I was my best companion.

Eggs Over Uneasy

JONATHAN AMES

Yesterday, I poisoned myself cooking three eggs. This is not an easy thing to do, but I managed to pull it off.

How did it happen? Well, I put the flame on beneath the frying pan and then got the butter and eggs out of the fridge. This may have been a mistake. The frying pan was too hot. When I put the butter on, it burned. Bubbled. Turned brown. Screamed out in pain.

But I ignored the screams and pressed on. Was too lazy to start over. I cracked three eggs on the side of the pan and dropped their yellow and white selves down into the brown grease. I wished I had organic eggs, but I consoled myself with the thought that the antibiotics in the eggs might be good during flu season.

The eggs immediately turned brown like the butter. A bad sign. But I ignored this sign. I flipped the eggs around a bit with my fork.

I put two pieces of thin German bread into the toaster. I

poured a cup of very dark, ink-black coffee, which I had made a few minutes before.

Usually, I do a tablespoon of coffee for every cup of water, but this particular morning I had emptied out the can of Cafe Bustelo because it was nearly finished and I can't bear scraping metal against metal—in this case, the spoon against the bottom of the can. Fingernails on a chalkboard, car keys against aluminum siding, coffee spoons in Cafe Bustelo cans, my father eating—there are certain sounds I simply cannot tolerate.

But the problem with my having dumped out the can is that it looked to be about ten tablespoons of coffee and I had only poured into the coffeemaker three cups of water. A ten-to-three ratio is probably not even practiced in Rome or Bogotá, but it seemed like the kind of coffee Philip Marlowe would drink. And I'm always game for playing the hardboiled detective. It helps make my semi-alcoholic bachelorhood feel rough and romantic.

It would have been nice to add a little milk to the cup of petroleum I was calling coffee, but I had sniffed the milk in my fridge and it was bad. I knew it would be rotten, but I sniffed it anyway. Why? Well, human beings often do things when there is no hope. For example, I'm always trying to flag down taxis that have their "occupied" light on. I see the light, register what it means, and yet I still wave at these unavailable taxis. In this way, it's like one's romantic life—we all want the cabs that won't stop for us.

So that milk was several weeks old, like everything else in my refrigerator. But did I throw it away? No. I'll probably sniff it again in two weeks' time, just to torment myself. I have two personalities. Two idiots. The one who sniffs the milk and doesn't throw it away, and the one who sniffs the milk two weeks later.

The inside of my fridge is more like a mortuary or a ring of hell (things dead and waiting for the next stage of the afterlife) than an icebox for edible foodstuffs. If you'll indulge me, I'm going to jot down a brief table-of-fridge-contents, as a way, perhaps, to show what kind of person I am (lazy and doesn't take care of himself):

1. Bouillon, capers, and an onion, all left by the French girls who used to live in this apartment six months ago.
2. A thickly congealed Paul Newman salad dressing bought during a very brief do-it-yourself-campaign—making salads and such.
3. Hardened organic peanut butter from my son's visit in October.
4. Two small containers of plastic applesauce forced on me by my great-aunt in Queens and taken from her meals-on-wheels package.
5. The aforementioned eggs, butter, milk, and German bread.
6. A container of expired orange juice (to keep the expired milk company).
7. A box of Cuban cigars—Cohibas, Castro's brand—that Angelo, my Italian movie star friend, smuggled back from Havana, and which I plan to give to my dad.

Well, thank you for indulging me. See how this fridge contents compares to your own. And now back to the riveting story:

I took a sip of the coffee and the toast popped. I buttered the toast, put it on a plate, and then I took the frying pan and tilted it over the toast. The brown, curdled eggs fell onto the bread. I then sat down at my kitchen table with the *Post* and my breakfast. I went to work with the knife and fork, while I read the gossip, the atrocities, and the sports. This was around ten-thirty A.M.

The next twenty-four hours is a blur of delirium and stomach pain. At first things weren't too bad, though. The caffeine caused mild psychosis and I found myself walking around my apartment and shouting "Motherfucker" a few times, which is interesting, since I'm not much of a curser and find it unattractive when others use vulgarities, but this caffeine-psychosis profanity was brought on, I vaguely recall, by going through my piled-up mail—a pile that has been neglected for two months—and being horrified at finding an invitation to a very nice party I had missed, as well as several enormous phone and credit card bills, all of which should have been paid weeks ago.

I also recall—though it's dreamlike because of the Cafe Bustelo—glancing at the pages of my new book, which had been sent to me by my British publisher for me to proofread. The Brits had computer-scanned the pages from the American publisher, and the scanning had created all sorts of strange typos. A classic, Joycean turn of phrase like "I let a fart leak out" had been turned into "I let a fart lead out." I thought of leaving that typo for a moment, as I sort of liked the idea of a fart leading somewhere, but then I changed my mind, thinking that the meaning of the sentence was too botched. And I realized after finding that typo that I was going to have to do more than just skim the pages. I was going to have to work hard and reread the whole damn book, *What's Not to Love?*, which is a narrative based on all the columns and articles I've written for the *Press* these last three, happy years.

The book will be in stores here in the States sometime in May, at which point my life will be seriously destroyed. It's one thing to write these self-revealing stories for the *Press*, where they're gone in a week and quickly forgotten, but it's another thing to have them put in a book, a book that will be around for a while and can be read by one's relatives. For example, future relatives like women who could be wives, but who will have nothing to do with me as the evidence mounts—three perverted books now—that I am too strange and damaged to be loved.

Anyway, the poisonous eggs and coffee had me in bed by two P.M., where I more or less stayed for the next twenty hours. The amphetamine-like coffee had overstimulated me and then I crashed. What happened to me was similar to that game at circuses that tests your strength—I was the weight and the coffee was the hammer and I went flying to the top, rang 'the bell, shouted "Motherfucker" for about an hour like a Tourette's sufferer, and then came sliding down, back to the bottom and went into a coma. I slept fitfully and with great nausea until about eleven P.M., and then I was up for hours with nauseous insomnia. I hate to vomit and so fought the urge all this time. For a few hours, I tried to read Wodehouse, usually a great pain reliever, and it helped some, but mostly, I lay there tormented, my stomach puckering like the overly fried eggs.

So I was clutching my pillow to my belly around three A.M. and felt quite alone in the world. Being by yourself and being ill can provoke despair, and so I indulged in Tom Sawyerish reveries of my funeral should this stomach ailment have proved fatal. It bothered me, though, that being Jewish, I'd be buried the next day and the service would have to be quickly put together and that many people wouldn't even know about it and would not come, making it a poorly attended performance. But I tried not to focus on this drawback of Jewish burial rites, and I selfishly imagined lots of weeping, crying, and impassioned, impromptu speeches. It was a way for me, on my faux deathbed, to feel loved. Pathetic, I know.

So what's the moral of the above tale? Well, I see two morals emerging: (1) I shouldn't cook for myself; and (2) I want to be loved. Now there's a perfect solution to both these issues: Go to restaurants. It may seem obvious why this solves number one, but it also solves number two, and that's because restaurants are staffed by waitresses. I've said it before, and I'll say it again: I have a great love for waitresses. No waitress has actually ever loved me back, but that's why I tip well—it's an act of courtship. I have this insane hope that if I leave a 30 percent gratuity that the object of my affection will think that I am a worthy suitor. And when I come across a waitress whom I greatly admire, I swear to myself that I will go to her restaurant for as long as it takes until we are man and wife or at least have a one-night stand.

But I've never followed through on these waitress courtships, except this one time a few years ago. There was this absolutely charming waitress in the East Village who had these translucent blue eyes and who always wore shirts that exposed one of the most beautiful stomachs in the Western world. So inspired by her eyes and belly (not to mention her very sweet personality and gorgeous face), I made a conscious effort, almost as a performance-art piece, to go to her cafe—a quiet little place—every Monday night for weeks on end (it was my treat to myself after teaching a fiction-writing class on Mondays). The secret rules of my endeavor were that I was to never make a flirtatious remark or go out of my way to have a conversation with her; if she wanted to speak with me that was fine, but I was to take no real action—all I could do was leave a handsome tip and behave like a gentleman. Well, after only four weeks, if she had a moment to herself, she started sitting at my table and would talk to me. I think she admired the way I always read a book with my meal. So a friendship began. She was from Spain and had come to New York to study film. We talked about movies and books.

Week seven, she hugged me goodbye and kissed me on the cheek when I left the cafe. I couldn't believe how well it was going. Week eight, she again hugged and kissed me—when I arrived and when I left! This was the greatest experiment of all time. By week nine, I was preparing to ask her out, but then outside the world of the cafe, I unexpectedly met a wonderful girl and we fell into an immediate serious relationship, and I abandoned the waitress.

Several months into this new relationship, almost as an act of infidelity, I went back to the cafe on a Monday night. My waitress beamed when I came in and my heart broke a little. Maybe I had chosen the wrong girl. And then while I was eating, a young handsome man came into the cafe and my waitress kissed him all over. She had a boyfriend, and this actually soothed my broken heart, because I thought to myself, as if taking a powerful aspirin, "It was not meant to be."

So there are a couple of reasons why I love waitresses. First of all they are often beautiful and men love beauty and are drawn to beauty. It can't be helped. Secondly, waitresses mimic the behavior of my mother—they bring dishes of nourishment to me. My mother was very much a 1950s mother and she served the family all our meals for years, thus creating this early association with love and the placing of a dish of food in front of me. (My mother also cooked the food, but I don't seem to love cooks; perhaps because I never see them.) And thirdly, I love waitresses because of the angle at which I observe them—I stare right into their asses and vulvas, two of my favorite spots, and when they bend over sweetly to warm my coffee, I catch glimpses of breasts, another all-time favorite spot. For example, my wonderful breakfast waitress in Brooklyn says to me all the time, "Do you want a warmer in your coffee, honey?" And she smiles at me when she says this; it's so lovely; and I say yes, and she bends over and I sneak a peek at her kind chest. I only see shadows, but it's enough.

Protective Measures

JAMI ATTENBERG

It started, as all self-indulgent habits do with me, in the midst of a failing relationship. I was twenty-five, drinking and drugging my way through the Capitol Hill neighborhood of Seattle, and desirous of something steady to hold me in place. He was twenty-seven, a pot-smoking recording engineer who had been raised to seek normalcy within an artistic life. He was the kind of man who calls you the day after a first date to tell you he had a nice time, even if you both got so drunk the night before you couldn't remember what happened. He also had a hairy back, so I thought he would never leave me, but that I could easily leave him. I will never get attached to this back, I thought, the first time my fingers became entangled in the hair. But the safer I felt, the more I fell for him; soon enough, he pulled away and he was working late, always working late, and the only time I would see him was: *late*. And it made me feel empty, as if he had taken two scoopfuls of my insides with his hands and hollowed me out. Then one Friday night, I'd had enough. If he wouldn't take me out on a date, I would take myself out. A movie, I thought. No, wait. *Dinner*.

I dressed up, which meant long unruly curls and a short skirt and black tights and Doc Martens, a baggy cardigan, and glitter on the eyelids. I smelled like incense, like something purchased on Broadway Avenue, a hundred sticks for two dollars. This was me being fancy. I was a ragged stoner rocker then; I was doing the best I could. I took a book and went down to Broadway, to the one sushi restaurant I could afford, the one in the mini-mall that had torn carpeting in the upstairs seating, which is where they wanted to put me, the table for one, but I insisted on sitting downstairs. I wanted people to *see* me. This was a declaration of independence. I liked the idea of being served. Someone out there was going to take care of my needs. I ordered a pile of sushi and rolls, fresh eel and tuna, California rolls. I indulged. Still young enough to hear echoes of feminist lit classes ringing in my ears, I read something by Margaret Atwood. I crossed and uncrossed my legs. I flipped the pages with great gusto. At home, I ate quickly, but here I was eating leisurely. I was daring some-one to see me alone on a Friday night.

At the end of the dinner, as I paid my check, I counted out a few extra singles, tipping harder than usual. It didn't matter that I couldn't afford it. In my world, a dream date ended with an outrageous tip (although ideally I would not be the one tipping). I stretched, finished my water, and strolled to the door. I rubbed my belly. Even if I was still alone, I felt *full*. The fullness and emptiness could somehow live side by side. I didn't feel lonely. Certainly, I was happier than if I had waited at home, miserable. If I had to be alone, this was the best way to do it.

A few weeks later I found out he was screwing a stage man-ager in her thirties who reportedly had a British persona in bed.

She said things like *arse* and *bum* in a Cockney accent, and she gave fantastic blow jobs. How do you compete with that? Still, I cried in his beat-up Toyota Tercel when he broke up with me, sad that I would never again tangle my hands in the wild tropical forest that grew on his back.

But I knew now that some kind of fullness could be attained by dining out alone. I'll show you who I am, I thought. I'm the girl who knows how to take care of her own needs since no one else knows how. Or is willing. I returned to that sushi restaurant many times on Friday nights over the next few years. I read a lot of books. I stuffed my face until I couldn't eat another bite. I was full. I was empty. I was learning how to survive.

After a while I started doing drugs alone instead of dining alone. It was a different kind of self-indulgence, but I was still spending money on something I didn't really need—Does anyone *need* to eat so much sushi her belly expands an extra size? Or to get so high she feels like her face is going to fly off?—but that I knew would make me feel special in some way. They were both highs of a kind, although one made me fat and one made me skinny. This was after I had left Seattle and moved to the East Village in New York in the hope of changing my life forever, which I did, although it has changed several times since then, as is New York's wont.

But first: I became slightly flush with dot-com money, all of which is gone now. In particular there was a summer when I consumed thousands of dollars' worth of cocaine, and I distinctly remember this was often in lieu of food. And while I did do it with friends on occasion, I enjoyed being alone on a Friday night, so that I could have it any way I wanted, whenever I wanted. At least until the bag ran empty.

Eventually, I took a trip to Jamaica to clean out my system. I know this seems preposterous, but all I knew about Jamaica was that people smoked pot there, and pot seemed to be a minor disturbance in my life compared with my all-consuming desire for cocaine. Plus, without any of my usual resources—no friends, no pager numbers—it might be easier to avoid. Of course, within five minutes of my arriving at Sangster International Airport, a boy approached me while waiting for my baggage and asked me if I wanted to buy drugs. He was probably about seventeen years old, and if I had let him, he probably would have tried to feel me up.

"We have to do it fast," I said. "I'm waiting for my bags."

The boy laughed at me. Those bags were going to take *forever*.

I went with him to his car, a two-door piece of tinfoil with a cardboard protector in the window to keep out the sun. He pulled out a few bags of pot in different sizes, the smallest of which still contained more than I could smoke in several months. I think it probably cost twenty-five dollars. I bought it. Encouraged, he pulled out a white sandwich baggie of cocaine. My heart leapt at the sight. I was sure the same math applied—all you could eat and more.

But I passed. The sun already felt so nice on my skin, like I was an egg heating up in a pan on the stove. Besides, the resort was all inclusive. I was most excited about the meals. It would be like a whole week of dates with myself. Everything was going to be just as I liked, and I was looking forward to eating again.

At the resort—one that I had specifically selected because it had no hedonistic selling points in the brochure—I checked in, drew a bath, and lit up a joint. I had stayed up too late the night before. I hoped I was sweating out every last drop of coke in my system, though of course I missed the irony of replacing it with another drug. (I missed a lot of ironies in those days.)

I took a pleasant walk around the grounds, took off my shoes and squished my feet in the sand, and then headed to dinner by myself.

The open-air restaurant glowed in candlelight, and at every table sat pairs of madly-in-love young couples, holding hands across the table, leaning in close, their fresh sunburns glowing against their stiff, new formal summerwear.

"Table for . . . ?" asked the maitre d'.

"One," I said, with slight uncertainty. I was just one, yes, but oh boy did I not want to be at that moment. How had I missed the fact that this was a romantic getaway?

I ate quickly, shoveled that food in my mouth, and got the hell out of there. It was one thing to be alone on a Friday night in a major metropolis. It was quite another thing to be alone in a room full of people hell-bent on romance. Proclamations of love would be declared that night. Marriage proposals would be made. Babies would be conceived.

No, I won't have any dessert or coffee.

The food barely filled me. I could have eaten forever, and I wouldn't have felt a thing.

.   .   .

The next morning I went to breakfast, in search of the smashing buffet of tropical fruits that the brochure had promised.

"Table for one, please," I said.

"Just one?"

"Just one."

I sat at the table, and the maitre d' promptly removed the opposing place setting. Minutes later, a waiter walked by, saw me with my lone place setting, and tried to set another one.

"No, it's just one," I said.

That I was forced to be insistent seemed unfair. I felt my "one" transforming into "alone." That was an entirely different sensation.

As I walked to the buffet, I passed sleep-deprived couples, still rosy with the memories of their morning copulation. I tried hard to ignore them, focusing instead on my destination, which was indeed smashing: a gigantic circular table piled with sliced mangoes and strawberries and oranges and pineapples, steaming trays of scrambled eggs and eggs Benedict and sausage and bacon and five kinds of bread, plus those little minibagels and English muffins *and* French toast—oh, they were so international!—all surrounding a lustrous flower display that burst forth from the center as if the flowers were fireworks on the Fourth of July, asking us to God bless America, although in this case, it was Jamaica.

When I returned to my table, the place setting had been restored; some anxious waiter unable to bear a half-dressed table, I suppose, had compulsively followed some training manual to the letter.

As soon as I put down my plate a waiter swooped on my coffee cup.

"Would he like coffee?" said the waiter, pointing to the cup across from mine.

"It's just one," I said firmly.

The place setting was once again removed.

I won't bother mentioning what happened when I went up for seconds.

I felt my heart sink into my gut. My morning buffet fantasy, crushed by the heel of a well-shined waiter's shoe! This game could not be played for a week, this "Who's on first?" for the solo female traveler. I would be devastated by the end of the trip, I knew it. I liked *choosing* to eat alone. I did not want to be reminded I had no other options.

So I took protective measures. For the rest of the trip, I ordered room service and ate in my hotel room. I would wake up in the morning, pick up the phone, and order an omelet or a fresh fruit plate and lots of coffee, please. Then I would smoke a joint from the never-ending bag of pot until the food arrived. Eventually I grew to hate that bag of pot. I was never going to be able to smoke all of it. And strangely, it was making me feel emptier.

Halfway through the trip I walked out onto the balcony of my room and emptied it. The green leaves flew into the sea air.

Now I live in the Williamsburg neighborhood of Brooklyn, far enough from Manhattan and my bad habits. My dates with myself are quieter now; drugs are no longer involved. The dates are no longer designed to attract attention, nor are they declarations of independence. Dining alone is simply a part my life, a ritual I can't imagine living without.

What I do is this: I buy a copy of *Us Weekly* (a magazine I usually read only on long airplane rides, when indulgence is necessary to get through the deadening claustrophobia), and I go to a restaurant in my neighborhood called Diner, a hipster-appropriated version of an original diner. They serve cheese-burgers but they also serve things like roasted beet and cucumber salad with ricotta salata. The members of the waitstaff could dou-ble as dirty downtown New York models. And probably are dirty downtown New York models. The food is always fresh, and they play great music, an on-point indie rock soundtrack, and there's plenty of eye candy, young and old (and by old I mean not yet forty) folks from the neighborhood. Usually they don't distract me from my magazine or meal.

There's a long bar in the center of the restaurant lined with comfortable leather stools perfect for the solo diner, although I sometimes I feel I'm sitting too close to the person next to me. We are all good at ignoring one another, though, the solo diners.

Sometimes I see someone from my apartment building. I live in a huge building, eleven floors, ten apartments or so on each floor, with an ever-changing influx of residents, artists, musicians, Europeans, and the occasional slumming advertising executive who wants to see what all the fuss is about with this neighbor-hood of ours. But it's the old-timers, the artists, who I know the best. We nod hello, not much more than that. It's fine. I'm here with someone. Me.

Once I talked to one of my neighbors, a guy in his late thir-

ties who lives a few floors up from me. He was sitting at one corner of the counter; I was on the opposing side of that corner. It's
the only way you can sit comfortably and have a reasonable conversation. I was drinking wine; his glass was full of a caramel-
colored liquor and some ice. I asked him about being an artist in
Williamsburg, as I was writing about that a bit at that time, and
he seemed suddenly eager to talk.

"I work mostly with metal," he told me, "but I do some film
work, too."

There was something faint in his voice, a far-off accent
scrubbed mostly away. I thought maybe he was Austrian. Or Dutch.
I knew we were both surprised to hear our voices out loud—I
hadn't spoken to anyone in a few days, except via e-mail—and we
talked carefully, testing them. It was nice to be heard.

And then I said, "You know, I've heard the art scene in
Williamsburg is kind of a boys' club."

And he cooled to me. I saw him recede. And I realized I had
fucked it all up. I almost always fuck it all up.

So mainly I sit and eat quietly. I smile at whatever bartender
is working, but never engage him (or sometimes her) in conversation. I tip well. I eat whatever I want, and I take as long as I
want, but I am usually in and out in less than an hour. It's just
enough time to please myself, to satisfy the urge to be served
and fed delicious food. I also want to make sure I'm connecting
with the world since I spend so much time by myself, scribbling
in my notebooks at home. But I know not to stay too long. I
eavesdrop too often. I notice happy couples coupling. Too long
and I'll wonder why I'm still alone.

This is not meant to mislead: I do not lead an empty life.

There is my work, there are my friends. Occasionally I busy my-self with falling in and out of love. But nothing quite fills me up like taking care of myself, taking care of my desires. Often the fullness lasts only for a minute, and then like the pain that comes from a pinch of skin, it is gone. But it's better than not having eaten at all.

Roasted Beet and Cucumber Salad with Ricotta Salata

1 bunch beets

Salt, to taste

Extra-virgin olive oil

Red wine vinegar

Freshly ground pepper, to taste

1 English cucumber

1 bunch radishes

¼ to ½ red onion

1 teaspoon chopped fresh dill (or more to taste)

1 teaspoon chopped fresh mint (or more to taste)

Ricotta salata

TO ROAST THE BEETS:

Remove tops and wash the beets. Place the beets in a roasting pan and sprinkle with salt and olive oil. Add a little water to the pan to prevent beets from sticking. Roast in 350° F oven until beets are easily pierced with a knife. Let cool, then peel off the skins and slice the beets into quarter-inch slices. Toss with a little vinegar, olive oil, salt, and pepper.

FOR THE CUCUMBER SALAD:
Make this at least half an hour before serving to let the vegetables soften. Peel the cucumber in alternating strips, then cut it in half lengthwise and scoop out the seeds with a spoon. Slice on the bias into quarter-inch slices. Slice the radishes into thin rounds. Cut the red onion in half and slice it as thin as possible against the grain. As with the beets, toss the cucumber, radishes, and onion with olive oil, vinegar, salt, and pepper as well as the dill and mint.

Place beets on the plate, put the cucumber salad on top of the beets, and shave ricotta salata on top.

NOTE: Recipe courtesy of Caroline Fidanza, Diner, Brooklyn, New York.

Table for One
ERIN ERGENBRIGHT

I wait tables in a restaurant at the hub of Portland's foodie culture, an industrial-chic destination spot where the chairs are hard and the food is fresh, local, and very fine, but not in a traditional fine dining way. There are no starched white shirts or black pants—it's all about the food. We've cultivated relationships with the people who grow and tend what we serve, and taken field trips to their farms, vineyards, and even to the slaughterhouse. To risk sounding like I have an altar to Alice Waters in the corner of my bedroom, I truly believe that a meal is the culmination of an entire journey from birth to death to table; a journey that includes, and is colored by, every person involved—not least the person who eats it.

But tonight, late, alone in my clean, white, and rarely cooked-in kitchen, I'm eating cold refried beans out of the can. And it's not the first time.

At clarklewis, the staff is fed incredibly well. At the end of a shift, the chef piles the carving table high with the surplus of our daily-changing menu. Tonight, for example, there was creamy

Anson Mills polenta; mesquite-grilled, locally raised lamb; bulls blood beets with gremolata; black cod with Prosecco butter; garlicky escarole; and braised fennel. We sit at a long wooden table to eat, drink, talk, and do our paperwork. Some of us have worked together for years. This communion sometimes takes on a heightened significance, the way eating with family can remind us of the thousands of times we've come together in the same way.

But tonight I didn't eat anything. My paperwork was snarled and frustrating, and I'd had a customer so determined to be and stay unhappy that I was now unhappy as well, and all I wanted was a glass of wine. Okay, two glasses of wine.

And hours later, I'm hungry and alone. Though the edge of my temporary unhappiness has been dulled by wine, my dinner options are revealed by the cold yellow refrigerator light— wilted lettuce, old eggs, a vast number of condiments, and a bottle of cold-pressed flaxseed oil. Sinclair, my fat, aging black cat, is sprawled across the piles of books and papers on my kitchen table, and I watch him stretch, carefully knock two books off the table, and then act startled. I laugh as I'm supposed to, then open the cupboard, the contents of which seem odd and inexplicable. Why do I have so many cans of creamed corn? Why do I have so many baking supplies when I haven't used my oven in over a year?

And then I see a can of Rosarita's vegetarian refried beans nearly hidden behind the whey powder. At the sound of the can opener Sinclair jumps off the table and weaves around my ankles. I let him sniff the beans' slick surface; he turns away. "I know. It's completely disgusting," I tell him, fishing a spoon out of the drawer.

Years ago, I read an article in a women's magazine that said self-care for singles should include a sumptuous meal made for you and only you, eaten on a table cleared of papers and letters and cats and set with a place mat, matching napkin, and a spray of bluebonnets in a vase. I don't remember which magazine it was, but I very well remember thinking, that's a perfectly lovely idea that's never, ever going to happen. And furthermore, why not a more easily procured flower, like a rose or a tulip?

But what was being espoused, of course, was the notion that you are valuable, *you alone*, and that beautiful, carefully prepared food is just as important for a table of one as a table of twenty.

And I agreed, in theory. But in practice, eating alone feels wrong. I'm so accustomed to eating with people, and serving people who are eating with people, that the social aspect of it seems inextricable from any other step on that journey from farm to table. Without the shared appreciation, a meal might as well not exist, like a book with no one to read it except the author.

And as I lean against the edge of the counter, eating my refried beans as quickly as I can to avoid really tasting them, I feel a rush of shame as I remember the very particular woman who ate alone at clarklewis three or four nights a week for nearly six months.

She was an immediate irritation to the staff. The first time she dined with us, she showed up six minutes before the kitchen closed and stood at the host stand impatiently, arms crossed in front of her chest. Her bare, unlined face suggested youth, but her floor-length skirt and sensible cardigan did not. I was disheartened: A single diner always means a lower check total, and she definitely didn't look like a drinker. And I'd thought my night was nearly over.

Single diners can be awkward. Some are lonely and want a lot of attention; some are nervous, embarrassed to be eating alone, and their discomfort is contagious. It's hard for me not to create a story around a single diner, as eating alone in a restaurant is an uncomfortable intersection between the public and the private. Serving the single diner I feel like a voyeur, and also guilty if I wonder why he or she is alone. After all, why is anyone alone, finally?

But this woman didn't seem lonely, nor did she want to be engaged. She simply wanted things exactly the way she wanted them. After I gave her one of the small flashlights we offer all our customers, as our restaurant is well-known for its rather intimate darkness, she demanded that I give her some of the votive candles from neighboring tables. Satisfied only after ten brightly burning candles illuminated her surroundings, she ordered room-temperature mineral water and then promptly returned her glass because it smelled of detergent. Her precision was strange and sort of gorgeous, and I was a little in awe of her as I brought her a new, neutral-smelling glass.

Our chef, however, isn't so awed by overly particular customers. Though exquisitely talented, he is equally mercurial, and occasionally prone to slightly hysterical, irrational behavior. And as I watched this woman pore over the menu with studious determination, I got a little worried. Every staff member has been, at least once, reduced to tears or silent rage by the chef's outbursts. I once brought a complaining customer's plate back to our open kitchen and whispered, "She says it's overcooked." Our chef's much too loud response was, "No, it isn't. You can tell her to go fuck herself."

Right, I'll tell her.

.   .   .

As I'd expected and feared, this very particular woman ordered three courses of items that were not on the menu. She wanted the shaved fennel and grapefruit salad, but she wanted the fennel to grapefruit in a ratio of three to one, and did not want our new-press olive oil dressing or the olive garnish or fleur de sel. She wanted the crostone of farm egg, speck ham, frisée, and aged balsamic without the toast or the ham, and with the egg as lightly poached as possible without being raw. She wanted the Fuyu persimmons without their accompanying heirloom lettuces or the Cypress Grove goat cheese. And she did not, and could not, tolerate garlic, and sent me back to the kitchen several times to see which meat and pasta courses could be prepared without it.

On this night, luckily for the garlic-intolerant woman, and therefore for me, the chef was in a good mood. Pleased with the experience, she returned the next day, and then every few days for the next six months. We came to refer to her as No Garlic Lady, and then, eventually, fondly, as NGL. (Once, and only once, NGL ordered something straight off the menu—as intended by the chef: a yellowfin tuna with heirloom tomatoes and oil-cured olive and caper salsa. The sous chef high-fived me. It never happened again.)

NGL adored food, and she ate with careful attention, apparently following her own formal set of rules and rituals, cleaning one small plate completely before touching the next. I found myself wanting to please her, to be as exacting as she was. She seemed to experience the kind of communion that I'd thought possible only with someone else to share in it. I started to look forward to seeing her. I always learned something about stillness and attention and self-care when I was around her.

Though excess conversation seemed to diminish NGL's experience, over time I learned that she lived in San Francisco and worked in computer programming. She often did business in Portland. When in Portland, she ate with us and only us. The one time she showed up when the restaurant was closed for a private party, she was disappointed in a way usually reserved for the discovery of infidelity. Each restaurant I suggested was met with a grimace. I worried about her—what would she eat? NGL was not the sort of woman who would eat refried beans out of a can.

So now, picturing her, I'm ashamed of myself. I set down my can and spoon and look around my midnight kitchen. Despite the papers and books and cats claiming the table, it is a calm place, abundant with plants. And as I rarely cook, the counters are very tidy.

I have a history of food allergies and eating disorders—years when food was not a pleasure, and was sometimes a source of near-despair—so despite my immersion in food and food culture, I often try not to think about what I eat. Sometimes, when I see people eating fast food or pepperoni pizza, I find it impossible not to imagine the conditions of a feedlot, or the screams of the downer cattle dragged to their factory slaughterhouse deaths. Even my mother tunes me out when I go on about this stuff, but I'm like a rubbernecker slowing past an accident—I can't help myself.

This is another reason I've preferred not to eat alone—conversation helps drown out thoughts of this sort of injustice, as well as the memories of deprivation, frustration, and being outside the norm. But now eating alone also reminds me of NGL, who is certainly outside the norm. Witnessing her has made these "dangerous" thoughts lose their sting. Of all the Portlanders I know who claim to be living in the present, of being in the *now*, NGL actually is: she eats with nothing between herself and her fine meal.

Though it may take practice to be as intentional and present as she is while eating alone, perhaps it's worth a try. I find my favorite green ceramic bowl and scoop the refried beans into it, remove the cat from the table, and put all the papers and books into a paper grocery bag. I find my favorite tablecloth, a green and yellow floral from Provençe, and place it over the painted wood. I locate an empty blue glass vase—I have a good imagination—to set in the middle of the table. With my pretty bowl of beans in front of me, I take a moment to focus before I begin to eat. They're still cold, true, but it's a start.

Yellowfin Tuna with Heirloom Tomatoes and Oil-Cured Olive and Caper Salsa
SERVES ONE

1 5-ounce yellowfin tuna steak
Sea salt and cracked pepper, to taste

2 heirloom tomatoes (like Brandywine, Marvel Stripe,
    or Cherokee)
1½ ounces oil-cured olives, pitted
1½ teaspoons capers in salt, rinsed
¼ bunch of basil leaves
½ lemon, zested and juiced
Pinch of red pepper flakes
¼ cup extra-virgin olive oil

Season the tuna steak with sea salt and cracked pepper, then set aside. Prepare the olive salsa by placing the olives, capers, lemon juice and zest, red pepper flakes, and olive oil in a small bowl. Mix well and set aside to let the flavors macerate.

You may pan sear the tuna steak in a very hot skillet over high heat with a splash of olive oil until medium rare, or grill the tuna steak over hot coals until medium rare. This takes about 3 minutes per side.

While the tuna is cooking, slice the tomatoes and place around your serving platter or plate. Season with a sprinkling of sea salt.

When the tuna reaches your desired degree of doneness, place on top of the sliced tomatoes, then add the basil leaves to the salsa, mixing lightly. Drizzle the salsa over the tuna steak and sliced tomatoes.

NOTE: Recipe courtesy of Morgan Brownlow, clarklewis, Portland, Oregon.

Wild Chili

DAN CHAON

When I was a child in Nebraska, my parents had a lot of parties. Friday. Saturday. Uncles, aunts, cousins, neighbors, my father's old friends from his job working construction, their wives and kids—thirty, forty people sometimes. They began to wander in around six or so, talking loudly, laughing, carrying coolers full of icy beer and pop. This was when my parents seemed the happiest.

Our house was about ten miles outside of town, a single-story, one-bedroom house that barely contained my family, let alone a party. The adults spread out through the rooms, drinking beer in the living room, playing cards on the porch, while the kids ran out of the house and across the yard to race through the large stubble field across the street. Set out on card tables were relish trays of radishes, green onions, slices of cheese and salami, pickled eggs, and jalapeños. The chili soup, barbecue meat, and tortillas would appear, eventually, after dark. Waylon Jennings, Willie Nelson, Crystal Gayle on the record player. Some people dancing in the little space between the couch and the TV.

I was the type of child who would sit alone at the kitchen table during the party—reading, writing, or drawing on a notepad, which I would guard with my forearms as if it were a test and there were cheaters all around me. While the other kids yelled and chased one another outside, while smoking, conversing grownups spilled into the room off the front porch where my bed and books shared space with the washing machine and the water heater, I staked out a little corner for myself, aloof from the action. I liked to be close to other people, observing secretly without really interacting with them, and in this way I was probably very much like my mother, who preferred cooking in the kitchen to dancing in the living room. I remember her lowering her head over the mouth of the pot as if whispering it a secret.

My mother made that Midwestern truck-stop variety of chili, which could be prepared in great quantities without much precision. It required tomato juice, browned hamburger, kidney beans, and yellow onions, chopped and sautéed. Salt, pepper, cumin, and chili powder were added "to taste," as my mother said. I loved to watch her experiment—sprinkle in a little of some spice into the pot, sample the broth, and then repeat, until it seemed correct to her. I still favor this method, though I have ruined a number of batches because of it, being too zealous with spices in the beginning, lacking my mother's restraint.

I moved from Nebraska to Chicago for college, and stayed there for a few years after graduation. Chili was one of the first meals I cooked, perhaps because it reminded me of those large family gatherings. But if it began with nostalgia, I soon discovered that chili had several other features that made it attractive to the young bachelor. It was a simple, inexpensive recipe that didn't require any particular organization or skill to prepare. It could be made by the gallon, and—like pizza and spaghetti—it could be eaten on a regular basis without ever really losing its appeal.

Cooking chili made me feel festive, even though I was alone in my apartment, as if I would soon be surrounded by a large group of happy people. And indeed, in time, making a big pot of chili gave me a reason to call some friends and have them over for beers. If I never managed my parents' kind of parties, I began to gather together a few other enthusiasts. No doubt, eating chili has male-bonding elements. There's that cowboy-on-the-range, bandito-in-his-hideout mythology lurking around it. And, of course—adding to its manly grit and ruggedness—chili can be extremely spicy.

And so spiciness, *heat,* was the first way that I varied from my mother's basic recipe. Back in Nebraska, we grew jalapeños and cayenne in the garden, which my father, grinning, would eat raw and which my mother pickled or made into salsa or dried and crumbled—*very* sparingly—into her chili, which was mild by all but the most grandmotherly standards. Now, living on my own, I could play around with the amount of chile pepper I used. In Chicago, I discovered a whole swath of hot peppers previously unknown to me, most notably the Scotch bonnet and habañero, but also the chiltepín and rocoto and Thai chiles, all of which I auditioned over subsequent years—on a few occasions creating monstrous stews of such indescribable heat that I could choke down only a few painful, burning bites.

As I experimented with degrees of heat and my own level of

endurance, I also became interested in straying beyond the standard ingredients. In this, I realize that I risk offending some fundamentalists for whom chili has an almost koanlike simplicity: a spicy chile-pepper broth with meat. Cook-off and Chili Society types even eschew beans.

I, however, have never been a purist. The best batches of chili I've ever made have had some unknown or incongruous element. In this way, cooking chili for me is not unlike the process of writing fiction, which requires the same openness to inspiration and possibility, as well as the same awareness that the final product may be irrecoverably different from what you'd first imagined.

Here are some of the things that I've put into chili over the years: African bird pepper, alligator jerky, artichokes, beer, beets, bourbon, carrots, celery, elk, epazote, fennel, garbanzo beans, green bell pepper, harissa, horseradish, hot dogs, Kahlúa, jicama, lavender, lobster, mango, red wine, spinach, turkey breast, vinegar, yeast, yogurt, zucchini.

When I was twenty-two, my friend B.P. and I had a quasi-mystical experience that involved the consumption of—and subsequent recovery from—several gallons of particularly potent chili.

I had spent the better part of that Friday evening and Saturday afternoon thinking about and working on this batch. The best chili needs to be created in solitude. It requires contemplative shopping and preparation, and perhaps it even requires us to exercise our ancient hunting, gathering, and foraging skills. This particular version involved some homemade spicy black-and-red-pepper deer jerky that my father had sent me for

Christmas, which I chopped into pea-sized pieces. Added to the simmering tomato juice, the jerky bits softened but retained just enough of a chewy texture to be intriguing. I stirred in a mixture of chorizo and hamburger, sautéed garlic and onion, a dozen purplish chile peppers (possibly purple habañero) purchased at a local Spanish market, several heaping spoonfuls of bitter Mexican cocoa, chili powder, cumin, oregano, cilantro, sweet corn, dark kidney beans, pintos, black beans, and green bell pepper. Adding item after item, purely by inspiration, was my favorite way to make chili. As items were added, I inevitably needed more broth. Sometimes, the broth became too thin and more meat, vegetables, and beans were then required. It became a complicated cycle—and led to the production of a massive quantity of chili when I had only planned on a meal for two. By the time B.P. arrived, the fifteen-quart stockpot was almost full. The lid clattered as the pot bubbled, and the small kitchen was wafting with the smell of spices that actually made the inside of the nostrils prickle. The chili was almost ready; finally, B.P. added some kind of psilocybin-containing mushrooms.

I have no idea how the two of us managed to eat all that chili, though I have a distinct memory of B.P.'s face, set in an intensity of determination that one sometimes sees in athletes as they push themselves past their breaking point. Dewdrops of sweat glimmered on his forehead. We sat on an ancient, boatlike thrift-store davenport, our bowls resting on old-fashioned TV trays that I found amusing and delightful—relics from the kind of suburban childhood I'd never had. B.P. had been a film major, and we thought of ourselves as bohemian, intellectual. We were watching Alain Resnais's *Last Year at Marienbad,* a French art flick, dreamily incomprehensible. A Mobius strip of murmurous Gallic dialogues competed with the noises of the city outside my apartment—sirens, hip-hop blaring from car speakers. The mushrooms kicked in. I was about as far from my mother's kitchen in Nebraska as I was likely to get.

That particular chili might have been the best I ever made. I imagined that it was an ideal combination of meaty savoriness, chocolate/cumin sweetness, and fiery spice, and I vividly remember the hypnotic mixture of textures—the doughy texture of pinto bean set off against the firmer kidney bean, the chewy jerky bits contrasting with the soft crumbled chorizo and hamburger. All of this was imprinted distinctly in my mind—even though when we groggily woke late the next afternoon, the chili, all three gallons of it, was gone, and (of course) I have found it impossible to re-create. Perhaps, ultimately, for the best.

As the years have passed, my desire to have my head blown off has gradually waned. I'm less impressed by the pure deadly power of a hot pepper, less interested in showing off my own prowess and endurance. I haven't turned my back on chili, but as I've moved further into my adult life—gotten married, had children, and so on—I do find that my relationship with it has become increasingly private.

Secretive, my wife says, and points out that most of the time I make chili when I am spending a weekend alone at home, when she and my sons are gone for one reason or another and I can spend undisturbed hours puttering around in our big three-story suburban house, like some eccentric middle-aged man with an enormous model train set in his basement.

I like to cook in the quiet of a late Saturday afternoon, the time of the weekend when, as a kid, I would sit at the kitchen table with my notepad and colored pencils; when, as a college student, I would laze alone in my dorm room making a collage or a mix tape. There's the same sort of hypnotic, slowed-time quality at work in stirring up some chili. Soaking the dried beans until they're soft. Sautéing some garlic and onions. Bisecting some strange new pepper I've discovered at the market. Stirring together powders and dried herbs and pastes of various sorts.

More often than not, by the time I'm finished I'll have once again made far too much for one person. More often than not, my wife and sons will come home from their weekend away and discover rows and rows of quart containers in the basement freezer, stacked and labeled and stored away, just like my parents used to do. I've chosen a much milder, more secluded middle age than they did. But I'm stocked up and ready, which I guess is yet another thing that I secretly take pleasure in. If hordes of people ever do show up at my door, I'll be prepared to feed them.

Dan Chaon's Chili
(Version #116)

1 cup dried dark kidney beans

1 cup dried pinto beans

2 pounds ground chuck

2 pounds hot breakfast sausage, bulk

4 jalapeño peppers, minced with seeds

4 poblano peppers, whole, seeded

1 large yellow onion, chopped

1 head garlic, chopped

46 ounces Spicy Hot V8 or other vegetable juice

2 cups beef broth

5 tablespoons standard dark chili powder

1 tablespoon unsweetened cocoa powder

2 tablespoons cumin

1 teaspoon ground black pepper

2 teaspoons sugar

½ teaspoon ground coriander

2 teaspoons chopped oregano leaves

¼ cup chopped cilantro

1 large red bell pepper, chopped and seeded

1 large tomato, chopped

2 teaspoons all-purpose flour

2 teaspoons cornmeal

2 tablespoons warm water

1. Prepare beans according to package, soaking them overnight. Drain and reserve beans.
2. Brown the hamburger and sausage. Pour off the grease; set aside the meat.
3. Sauté the jalapeño and poblano peppers, onions, and garlic until onion is translucent, about 7 minutes.
4. Mix beef stock with vegetable juice and all spices. Bring to a boil over medium-high heat.
5. Add the beef, sautéed vegetables, and beans. Lower the heat. Simmer on low for about two hours, stirring occasionally.
6. After the chili has cooked for about 1¾ hours, add bell pepper and tomato.
7. Stir together flour and cornmeal; add warm water. Mix well. Stir into the chili and cook, covered, for another 20 minutes.

White-on-White Lunch for When No One Is Looking

ANNELI RUFUS

She was *so* angry.

She grabbed me by the shoulders and pushed me up against the wall, in the foyer just inside our front door. I'd just come in. The back of my head banged against the wall with its green-gold wallpaper textured to look like bamboo. Two balsa-wood masks swung on the nails that moored them. My mother's face was inches from mine, her thumbnails digging half-moons into my skin through the thin fabric of my T-shirt.

I don't know which T-shirt. Only that because this was happening in Los Angeles, in summer, it had to be a T-shirt. I had worn it to go and see my friend Laurel, who lived across the street. Laurel was having company, *other* company, her *other* best friend from the *other* town where her family lived before moving to L.A.—so when I heard their car pull up after returning from the airport, I rushed over and met this Tamara, already eleven, with her wavy blond bangs, under the false-orchid tree that shed purple blossoms shaped like sailboats.

But after half an hour or so I caught them exchanging looks that meant *Get her out of here!*

The masks went *clack-clack* on the wall. My mother drew closer as if we were going to kiss, which of course we were not. She sniffed—making a sharp sound like scraping cement.

What did you eat?

Digging her sandaled heel into the hardwood floor. *What did you eat?*

Nothing. I said it way back in my throat, like a ventriloquist, so that as little air as possible escaped my mouth. But *sniff sniff*—pepper. Nitrites. Smoke and vinegar.

She always said liars are worse than thieves. She said it then.

Her thumbnails, ow.

Her eyes raced down my face, my front, as if it were made of clear glass and she could see inside. She knew.

Hot dog.

It was always worst when she growled like that. Like God. She pronounced it her own way: *doh-wug.*

Over at Laurel's, there had been this box of hot dogs her family had bought at Der Wienerschnitzel on the way home from the airport, where they picked up Tamara. They were like that, picking up fast food, throwing banana-split parties, ordering pizzas on whims. And her mother had lifted plump cylinders out to all of us: *Who wants a mustard dog? Who wants a kraut dog?* And I should have said no thanks as usual. I should have said *I have to go.* But that would have meant going. Leaving Laurel here to play Barbies with Tamara. And I was not going to go until they forced me out. Which they did, like ten minutes later, but not before that mustard dog.

Heat rose in waves off Mom's face.

My dad passed us en route to the kitchen, carrying a wrench: *What's going on?*

She poked the soft spots right above my collarbone for emphasis. *She went. Across the street. And ate a hot dog.*

But *doh-wug* made it sound nastier, like something that waggles and gleams.

She had this rule, and it was: never eat at other people's houses. No matter what they said. No matter what they did. No matter what they offered, decline. Either tell them the truth—*Sorry, not allowed*—or depending on who they were, come up with a lie. *I have a stomachache. I'm allergic to frosting. I'm not hungry,* though this last one was difficult because I was hungry all the time. My mother served three meals a day, real meals with meat, but between them I was racked with a wild, aching hunger, though Mom said *You're not hungry, you're just bored.*

No, I'm hungry.

I know you. You're bored.

At home she served no snacks. Nor could I sneak them from the fridge—she could hear footsteps on the kitchen lino from the far end of the house, even with Merv Griffin on TV interviewing psychic mediums and acrobats. She would hear fingers riffling through the sock drawer where my father hoarded candy: giant Hershey bars, boxes of Dots, pound bags of chocolate Santas or marshmallow peanuts that he was allowed to eat but I was not.

Anyway, this rule. She said I shouldn't eat what others offered because if I did, they would think I was starving, that I wasn't being fed enough at home. If I ate what they gave me they would have a chance to observe my manners and remark on them. If I ate what they gave me they would laugh behind my back—after I left, they would point at my empty plate or soiled napkin and snicker to one another: *What a hog!*

And most of all, the main thing was that eating other people's food would make me fat.

Mom was watching my weight. I was thin in a flat, unremarkable way, but she watched me in my school clothes and play clothes, in my swimsuits and the giant mirrors at the mall. She checked on me in the bathtub on the pretense of asking whether or not I had a towel.

She watched, because life is so cruel. She watched, because my three best friends were overweight and what if I became like them? Like proselytizers, how could they resist? Either in innocence, because they loved their fudge and Cheez-Its and wanted to share this joy—or in contrivance, loathing their own weight and seeing my flat bottom as a mockery. A taunt. They thrust corn-chip bags at me like maracas, *cha-cha-cha.* They snatched boxes of Jell-O off the shelf, saying *Let's suck the powder straight out of the box with straws.*

She knew.

Mom was once fat herself, as a big-city schoolgirl whom the other kids called Four-by-Four and Blubberjug and Tub. She knew. Back in those days—see her in pictures, seersucker and taffeta stretched tight as sausage casings, scowling at the lens as if its glass could laugh.

Not that she was still big or anything. A life-threatening illness at age thirty sheared her down to a size ten and there she stayed. But by God she must watch me. Anything might inflate me at any moment, one French fry or jellybean too many. For those hours when she was not there to see: the rule.

My friends scoffed at the rule. Their parents scoffed. *Honey, that's silly!* My friend Karen's mom was Japanese. She called my mom and put on a fake accent, saying *Plea-zu can she su-tay heah for lunch. Ho-su-pitality is the Jah-panese way.* No luck. Another day, my friend Michelle's dad—he was drunk—called my mom demanding that she let me share his daughter's Ritz crackers. *So you're kosher, so what?* he boomed. *It's not like they're pork rinds.*

No, but they were crackers, and crackers were the worst food of all. Crackers, cookies, bread, cake. I mean, all food was treacherous just because it was edible, but my mother had special theories about starches being the most treacherous of all. Eating a hot dog across the street was bad enough—and she was in a red-cheeked rage from it, though really it was all from love—but she would not have jammed her thumbnails into my shirt if it had been just a frankfurter without a bun. I almost could have talked my way out of it, said it was a new Der Wienerschnitzel product, a special sales promotion: the new bunless low-calorie dog. I should have said so outright, but by the time I thought it up, it was too late, would have been obviously a lie, because buns made so much difference that if there wasn't one, then by God that's the first thing you would mention. She sometimes forgave me, hours later, for eating fried chicken. Fish sticks. Even ice cream. But not ice cream in *cones.* Never chicken with *biscuits.* My mother was an Atkins dieter before there was an Atkins diet, back when Dr. Robert Atkins was a plain old cardiologist who recommended vitamins. She said that even sugar was better than starch because sugar was a source of *quick energy,* which bodies could *burn off* if they played hard. Rolls, on the other hand, or spaghetti, were sneaky. They turned into glue when you chewed them and they slid inside you and adhered. Layer on layer—stuck.

Bread was never served with meals at our house, and at restaurants we shunned the rolls or Saltines that came free: we ate huge quantities of meat and salad, even bowls of ice cream for dessert, even with slabs of Dream Whip. We had cereal or bagels now and then for breakfast, but a nimbus of sin and foreboding hung over them. *Someday you'll pay for this!* In my school lunches I got beef sticks, or hot soup in Thermoses, and sometimes sandwiches but on a special thin brown "dietetic" bread. I straddled the bench eating my sandwich, its dietetic bread framing six slices of bologna, piled half an inch high, as Laurel laughed, eating a Ding Dong, white cream spurting through the gap between her teeth.

When I went away to college in another town, my residence card gave me access to a dining commons three times a day, where buffet meals were served. Mom was worried, and rightly so. But I did not rebel. Tray after tray of fresh bread and lasagna and German chocolate cake lined the stainless-steel rack that gleamed into the distance like a runway. Other freshmen grew fat. I forked lettuce into my mouth, thick with Thousand Island dressing, nibbled bunless patties, and poured so much Sweet'n Low into iced tea that it tasted of deodorant, or zinc.

After two years in the dorm, I shared an apartment with friends. I worked at a frozen-yogurt shop, so my junior and senior years were fueled almost entirely on frozen yogurt—plain or with cashews. One night at the frozen-yogurt shop I met a classics major with hair the color of pennies. I gave him a free cone, not that night, of course, but the next, and the next and the next.

We were in Europe together after graduation, drifting hand in hand for months through Viking theme parks and wallpaper museums and chapels constructed of human bones. Of course, I was still eating my same way, ordering steaks and half-chickens and saucissons, shunning the baskets of bread, rolls, and pastries that came with meals and gleamed in bakeshop windows. Brioches and croissants. German seeded spirals served with tiny tubs of liverwurst. Golden Austrian crowns awaiting jam. Dark Dutch gingerbread, oil-jeweled Spanish churros shaped like wands: under the dry blue sky he dipped his in hot chocolate, pudding-thick. *I'm not hungry,* I said. Ten thousand bakeries where he chose tarts and loaves and puffs: and then one day . . .

I still wonder what it was about *that day*. It was not a birthday or a holiday, just a plain Wednesday or Sunday. We were in Delphi, that Greek hill-city where ancient sibyls used to read the future in smoke that rose up swirling between their feet from cracks in the soil. That midmorning he took his time in the bakery, eyeing its racks of honey-soaked baklava and syrupy shredded-wheat nests cradling nuts. But no. Handing the clerk his few coins, he chose two raisin rolls. Plain. Round. The slick brown of saddles.

Try one, he said when we were outside, on a bench in the clattery street with its view of the slopes whose pine and juniper mixed with the traffic perfume. He held it out to me on his freckled hand.

Ha ha, I said, *no.*

Try it, he said, biting the other one.

What was it? The black coffee we'd been drinking all morning from tiny cups? The proximity of sibyls? The fact that I was farther from home than ever before? Almost without thinking—*almost* but not quite: I felt a flash, a reconnaissance, as you feel at reunions—I took the roll and ate it. Just—pulled off one tuft after another and put them into my mouth till it was finished. That stretchy softness, warm to the teeth, black fruit off mountain vines popping like music.

More than twenty years have passed since that roll. I kept the guy, but otherwise I've never looked back. After that trip I found out that I've always been hypoglycemic. My blood cannot produce enough of its own sugar, and aches for it. This is why I've always gotten so hungry between meals, that pounding demented hunger. My blood screams *please please please mainline complex carbohydrates,* with their linked sugar molecules like strings of beads regulating the glucose, drop by drop, to calm me. *Moron, give me that,* it says—it said for all those years, but I cursed it. All those uneaten Cheez-Its spilled on the ground, wasted bliss. But no longer.

I crave starch. I eat it. Pastries, French fries, and bread produce a kind of euphoria, a floaty sparkly electrical charge. I eat sponge cake. Noodles. Toast.

And the plainer the better, those thick butterless slices, barely toasted, those noodles tossed only with cottage cheese. I am like an alcoholic drinking straight shots. My copper-haired guy laughs at my enthusiasm. I like these foods more than he ever did, in the same way that converts are the most devout daveners in the shul.

He likes spicy dishes. Salty dishes, soupy dishes, crunchy dishes. He likes mixed dishes in which the starch is dotted or even overwhelmed with other items. When we are eating together sometimes we go my way but sometimes we have to go his.

Sometimes I have the whole house to myself. When he is not looking, when he is not awake or is off playing chess and cannot laugh at me, it is plainest of all: white on white and nearly dry, without a trace of spice. He cannot laugh when I toss noodles with cottage cheese. My mother lives five hundred miles away and cannot watch me eat. When we see each other, she praises me for staying almost the same weight as when I was in high school. I think she might even take credit for that. She has watched me polish off a pot of white rice and sat squinting, as you might at a magic trick. Tossing together pale ingredients now in the empty house—the radiant yield of wheatfield and cornfield and rice paddy and potato patch—I mutter: *I'm making up for lost time!* If I do it fast enough, the copper-haired guy who dreams of vindaloo and chipotle and kimchee will not see. He cannot laugh as he likes to do, pitying my food for being plain. He cannot say it is a kind of crime: a waste, chicanery, as some say about those white-on-white paintings by Mark Rothko.

White-on-White Lunch for When No One Is Looking

1 12-ounce package egg noodles

2 cups cottage cheese

Salt and/or pepper, to taste (optional)

Cook noodles in boiling water as directed on package. Drain in colander. When dry, toss with cottage cheese. Add seasonings if you like, though I never do. It is possible to dress this lunch up by adding canned spinach and garlic, chopped fine. But that would distract from the noodles.

Luxury
HOLLY HUGHES

Eating alone? Ah, that would be luxury.

Cooking alone? That's an entirely different thing—that I do every night.

Or to be more precise, every night I am the only person in my kitchen whose activities are directed toward producing a meal for group consumption. There are other people in the kitchen, all right, but they are busy doing homework, or playing with the cat, or watching *Jeopardy*, or sneaking snacks to spoil their appetites, or arguing with the cook (me). They never offer to help with the cooking. No, they are simply hanging around, bored, at loose ends, just waiting to be fed.

"What are you going to put on that chicken?"

"What would you like me to put on that chicken?"

"I hate it when you do the tomato sauce."

"Then what would you *like* me to put on that chicken?"

"Remember the time you made it with sweet peppers and onions?"

"Want me to do that again?"

"I specially hated it with the peppers and onions."

[SECOND VOICE FROM THE LIVING ROOM, OVER THE NOISE OF PIANO SCALES] "Oh, yeah, do the peppers and onions again! That was awesome! Do we have red or yellow peppers?"

"I have green peppers."

[SCALES STOP] "Yuck! Green peppers? Those make me wanna puke!"

Nobody asks—nobody is going to ask—what *I* would like on the chicken. But if they did . . .

Mushrooms. Yes, definitely mushrooms. I am the only person in this family who will eat mushrooms, and so I never get to eat them. And oh, God, I miss them. Lovely thin slices of portobello mushrooms, delicately simmered in marsala, layered over the top of a perfectly sautéed boneless breast of chicken. Or no, wait, a boneless breast of chicken stuffed with mushrooms, water chestnuts, and oysters. Something not found in any recipe book, something I would make up myself, a culinary experiment, just puttering around the kitchen on a long leisurely afternoon. Something that would take hours to prepare, slicing and dicing and marinating and adjusting the spices. I wouldn't even care if it tasted good, just so long as I could use the ingredients I wanted, every last exotic one of them. And sit down to eat it *in peace.*

The first time I ever properly ate alone was August 8, 1974. Richard Nixon was due to go on television that night to announce his resignation. My parents, the staunchest of staunch

Republicans, had gone out to some party with my younger sister. I stayed home—I wouldn't have missed that historic night for anything. I made a Special Occasion Meal: eggs Florentine, which I'd discovered at a restaurant in London the previous summer.

I had no recipe, but how hard could it be? I carefully steamed my spinach, poached my eggs, covered it with freshly grated Parmesan. I had a fresh baguette (not easy to find in Indianapolis in 1974, I can tell you) and a glass of dry white wine. I sat down at a TV tray in our den and turned on the momentous broadcast.

I felt like a grown-up at last: I had my own political opinions; I had the right to drink wine. And I was capable of cooking for myself.

When I first had a baby, my husband and I still ate interesting food. The baby was content to have yummy slop spooned to him, though never out of jars—I puréed my own, thank you very much. I took time with the meals I prepared for my husband and me—or for myself, if my husband was working late. That didn't count as eating alone, because there was an adorable baby, the cutest the world had ever seen, in the room with me.

When the baby graduated to solid food, I was excited at first about the prospect of introducing new foods to my child. I'd pick up the kitchen phone and call my husband with the news, like dispatches from the war zone.

"The peas are a hit!"

"He likes the poached salmon!"

"You should have seen his face when he tasted the sautéed leeks!"

And then I pushed my luck too far. Couscous—what toddler wouldn't like couscous; it's just baby-sized pasta, right? . . . Well, have you ever tried to surgically remove an entire dumped plateful of couscous from a wicker chair seat?

The grilled fish, mesclun salad, and wild rice gradually morphed into fish sticks, carrot sticks, and Rice-A-Roni (the San Francisco Treat!). A second child was born, and I now faced the task of cooking three meals a night—one of puréed slop, one of buttered pasta and chicken fingers, and one ragout of rabbit forestière. Three meals was obviously too many. One had to go. Guess which one went?

My husband works late much more often now. Hmmm. Not that I blame him, considering the kinds of meals he could expect if he did hurry home.

"Mommy, why is the meat so crusty?"

"Yuck, Mom, why is the rice so slimy?"

"Mom, this has boogers in it."

The answers are simple:

1. The meat is crusty because you were teasing your brother, and while I was trying to stop World War III, I forgot and left the meat in too long.

2. Marcella Hazan told me you'd like that slime in the rice.

3. Boogers give you protein—eat them all
   up now.

None of which makes me feel any less guilty when I see them wolfing down goldfish and graham crackers half an hour after they supposedly ate dinner.

If I didn't know the people I was cooking for—if I were, for example, a chef in a restaurant—I wouldn't have to take their tastes into account. But, oh, I know them, I know them very well. I know that Tom won't eat any cheese except for grated Parmesan, which he must grate himself. The only fruits Grace will eat are bananas, raisins (but not the grapes they are made from), and apple juice (but not the apples it is made from). Hugh is okay with fish—well, salmon, at least—but the others think it's poison, so if I cook fish (meaning salmon), I have to make another entrée for the non-fish-eaters.

Fish. Oh, fish. Please, not salmon for once, but a lovely fillet of red snapper, lightly grilled, with a fine dusting of Cajun spices on top. Served on a bed of wild rice (with just a kiss of slime), and butternut squash on the side, puréed baby-food smooth. On a real china plate, not a scarred melamine plate with the Powerpuff Girls ka-powing around the rim. I wouldn't even need wine, not really; I'd be content with mineral water, chilled just enough to frost the sides of a crystal goblet. And maybe a little music in the background ... some Coltrane would be nice ...

And come to think of it, I don't even want my husband home for this. No sirree, he is not invited. This is a party for one. He'd want to talk about his day at work, and I do not want to talk. I want all the talk, all the chatter, all the YAMMERING, all the HOLLERING—to cease. I want to listen to the Coltrane, and savor the food in silence—every chewy grain of rice, every velvety slurp of purée, every sip of the pure clean cold water, every moist flaked morsel of fish.

Well, they did eat fish at one time. Sorta. There was that tuna pasta salad I used to make—my own recipe, a riff on something I had at a luncheon once, with canned tuna and cooked pasta, garnished with chunks of raw bell pepper and canned mushrooms, seasoned liberally with grated Parmesan and bottled vinaigrette. In desperation, I threw this salad together for the kids one night and to my great surprise they fell in love with it. Refinements crept in over the months—tricolor rotini became the pasta of choice, only yellow and orange bell peppers could be used (the green ones make them puke, remember?)—but those were questions of shopping, not cooking. This dish was easy to make and a reliable crowd pleaser.

Tuna pasta salad had one other huge thing to recommend it—it could be Made Ahead of Time, a perfect solution for the nights when a teenage babysitter was coming over. Efficient Chef Mom whips up a delectable and healthy tuna pasta salad before the babysitter gets there, and dinner is literally a snap. Picture me in my June Cleaver starched shirtwaist with pearls and a frilled apron, snapping my manicured fingers.

So of course, I couldn't resist. I made tuna pasta salad every time my imagination faltered—which, face it, got to be pretty damn often. Until one night I heard the dreaded words:

"Oh, no, not tuna pasta salad again!"

I began to see larger and larger mounds of the pasta left to grow cold and cement itself to the edge of their plates. Tom came to the amazing realization that tuna pasta salad contained tuna, and he began to pick out the shreds of tuna from around every whorl of the pasta (shells, rotini, you name it—no pasta shape was concave enough to hide tuna from the prongs of his fork). At long last, tuna pasta salad was removed from the active roster, its number retired, its jersey hung in the rafters.

I'm not even going to try liver.

My mother made awful liver. It tasted like shoe leather, and we only had it once, when I was six; we all spit it out on our plates and that was that. The Great Liver Rebellion had a profound impact on my young mind: I resolved that I would never make my children eat something they hated.

I will have to say, I did eventually eat liver again. In graduate school, I was invited to dinner at a professor's house and we were served liver—which took amazing nerve on the part of that professor's wife, I thought. But this wasn't just liver, it was thin scallops of calves' liver, exquisitely sautéed with a glaze of soy sauce and wine, and it melted in my mouth. From this I deduced (a) that my tastebuds might have matured since I was six, and (b) that my mother was a rotten cook.

I immediately went and taught myself how to cook liver that

way. When I was a young single, in my first apartment, I cooked it many times. I learned all the secrets my mother never knew, about buying the right cut from the butcher and timing the sautéing just right. I discovered that liver went very well on a bed of brown lentils and chopped roasted carrots. I could cook it so that it melted in my mouth, that silky texture, that earthy savory taste. When I cooked it for myself, I made sure to sit at the table, light candles, and have a really good book to read while I dawdled over my meal, eventually polishing off every lentil, every speck of carrot. It was a perfect way to leave the office behind, to say to the world, *I am a grown-up. I don't have any papers due. I didn't bring any work home tonight. My evening is mine.*

I could never cook it for my children. I just couldn't bear it if they spit it out.

I used to think the situation would improve once my children started to develop a palate. Well, they're developing palates, all right—they've decided, for example, that the chicken cutlets I make myself, breaded with a mixture of fresh breadcrumbs and freshly grated parmesan cheese, are infinitely better than the Tyson frozen chicken patties they used to get. No matter that Mom has to separate eggs and beat the whites to a froth to coat the chicken before dredging it in the breadcrumb mixture; no matter that she has to lovingly tend the frying pan while said breaded cutlets are swiftly browning to a not-quite-crisp state of perfection. The homemade chicken cutlets are better, that's all they know.

Well, yes, of course the homemade chicken cutlets are better.

Anyone could taste that—anyone with a palate, that is. I prefer the homemade ones too. But now I face a half-hour of intensive labor instead of the fifteen seconds it used to take to toss the frozen slabs into the toaster oven. No wonder I don't feel like I'm making any progress.

I'm not much of a mathematician, but even I can calculate the inverse ratio between the amount of time it takes me to cook a meal for them and the amount of time it takes them to eat it. Laboring over made-from-scratch macaroni and cheese makes no sense when they swill it down as fast as they do the stuff from the blue box. (Either way, I have to make two batches, one macaroni with cheese and one macaroni without cheese, for Tom, the no-cheese-eater.)

Not that I have anything against the stuff from the blue box. There is a time when mac-'n'-cheese from the blue box totally hits the spot. You know what? Canned ravioli hits the same spot—that place at the back of your throat where a glut of salty or sweet or glutinously gummy food jams up for a moment and you feel gloriously sated. All right, I'll admit it, swilling it down is the preferred method of eating this sort of guilty-pleasure food. You just keep shoveling it in, and all the synapses start to buzz and the endorphins come a-rushing, and all's right with the world. For at least four and a half minutes.

And that rush, too, is best enjoyed alone, damn it.

One summer night, at a cottage we were renting on Cape Cod, the woman who lived next door mentioned to me that she was going to be alone for a few days. Her husband and teenage son worked in Boston during the week. Eager to be the good neighbor, wanting to make sure she wasn't lonely, I invited her over for dinner with me and my three small children.

She gave me such a look. "Why, uh, thanks ... but you know, I think I'll just stay in."

"No, but really, I have this big ham I was going to cook—"

She grinned. "But I was looking forward to it, actually. Sometimes you just need to curl up with a plate of scrambled eggs all by yourself. I never get to do that. It's like heaven. You know what I mean?"

Well, I didn't until she said it. And there hasn't been a day since then that I haven't thought wistfully of that plate of solitary scrambled eggs.

"Mom, can I stay at Amanda's through dinner? Her mom can drop me off at eight. We did our homework together. Please, Mom?"

I do rapid calculations. Dad is working late again. One brother has an away wrestling meet and won't be home until seven-thirty. The other one has two friends in his room, working on a team project; they ordered pizza an hour ago.

Still cradling the phone under my chin, I yank the chicken nuggets out of the toaster oven so fast I burn my fingers on the pan. "I guess so, honey," I tell her, trying to sound sorry. I hang up the kitchen phone with a clatter. Dropping the chicken nugget pan into the sink, I bump open the pantry cupboard with a spare elbow. No blue box, no canned ravioli. I nudge open the fridge with my burned fingers. What did I expect?—there are no mushrooms in there, no fish, certainly no liver.

But there is, oh hallelujah, a carton of eggs.

Luxury.

Eggs Florentine à la Mom

SERVES ONE.

6 cups fresh spinach leaves

1½ to 2 tablespoons butter

1 tablespoon flour

½ cup heavy cream

½ teaspoon sugar

3 large eggs

Salt and pepper, to taste

Wash and clean spinach leaves and place in a steamer. While the spinach is steaming, melt butter in skillet. Measure flour. Discover a colony of mealworms in the flour, escapees from the kids' most recent science project. Try to pick mealworms out of the flour before stirring it into the butter. Remove cream from the fridge, smelling the carton just in case. Look at the expiration date. Throw carton into trash. Decide to go with steamed spinach instead of creamed spinach.

Prepare to poach eggs. Look for the egg poacher. Discover that it is now coated with purple acylic paint from last spring's egg decorating project. Spend fifteen minutes trying to chip the paint off the poacher.

Snatch the steamer off the burner just in time to prevent major kitchen fire. Check inside pot. The same scouring pad you have been using on the poacher can also be used to remove the incinerated spinach from the steamer.

Rinse out the skillet and melt some more butter. Consider breaking eggs into a small mixing bowl. Decide you have enough washing up to do already. Break eggs directly into the skillet, scrambling them with your spatula as they cook. Salt and pepper liberally.

My Favorite Meal for One
PAULA WOLFERT

In 1961, while in my early twenties, I lived for about a half a year in Paris at the now-legendary "no name hotel" on rue Git-le-Coeur. The halls smelled of marijuana, garlic, cheap frying oil, and Gauloise cigarettes. Brion Gysin lived across the hall, and William Burroughs lived in a tiny back room on the floor below. The poet Gregory Corso provided the place with its legendary name: the Beat Hotel.

I was attracted to the bohemian lifestyle, but theirs was a gay or guy thing, so I was never really welcome in their circle. There were plenty of other younger poets, painters, and jazz musicians staying at the hotel to befriend.

My room, number 23, had a small two-burner gas stove in the corner that ran on a meter. I often used it to cook an evening meal (a hearty soup), which I then shared.

Once in a while, I ate alone. Then, in want of companionship, I'd go downstairs to the bar to chat with whoever was hanging around. Most often I'd talk to the concierge, Madame Rachou. She was so short that she had to stand on a wooden crate behind the bar in order to serve coffee. She had blue-white hair and loved the American and English writers and artists who inhabited her hotel—not the usual response to Anglos in Paris at that time.

When just the two of us were together in the bar, she'd refer to me sympathetically as *toute seule*—all alone. How I hated that expression, expressing, as I thought it did, pathetic lonely datelessness. Perhaps my face revealed how I felt, for often she would sit down opposite me at one of the small tables and share some gossip. When she found out I was interested in food, she described the rich hare ragout and bean and lamb stew she'd cooked and served in the café when her husband had been alive.

Those evenings were my first real experiences with solitary dining, and eventually I came to like it. So what if I sometimes ate *toute seule?* I was young, living in Paris, and my whole life lay ahead.

I have a food-writer friend who eats lunch alone every day in his Manhattan apartment. In the evenings, he goes out to eat with friends. He makes a ritual of his solitary lunches. After he prepares a dish, he takes off his apron and changes into a jacket and tie. He sits down at his table, which has been set with his best sterling silver and china. He puts a freshly ironed cloth napkin on his lap.

Although I admire his approach, my own solitary meals are nowhere near so ritualistic or formal. Still, I've come a long way from eating *toute seule* in a drab room at the Beat Hotel. These days, when I eat alone, I try to make the experience at least a little bit grand.

A few years ago, in Barcelona, I purchased a special plate. It's one of a kind and so I only use it when I dine alone. It's earthenware, glazed a rich yellow with a green and red-brown rim, and there's lettering on it.

This lettering is my inspiration: *Pa amb Tomàquet* reads one line. In the middle of the plate there's a circle containing an "i," and at the bottom, the word *Pernil*. In the Catalan language this means "Bread with Tomato . . . and Ham." And that, if I can find all the correct ingredients, is my favorite eat-alone dish.

For me *pa amb tomàquet* sums up all that is best in the Mediterranean, an area whose cuisines and flavors I've been studying my entire adult life. This same basic combination appears in numerous Mediterranean lands. Good sea salt and extra-virgin olive oil are the only other essential ingredients.

I've written before about a version my husband and I ate as a beach picnic on the Greek island of Paxos. There the country-style bread, *frigania,* was sun-toasted, the local oil had a faint overtaste of hazelnut, the air was balmy and bore the aroma of wild herbs and spring wildflowers, the light slanted just perfectly through the olive trees behind us, and we were soothed by the gentle sounds of the Ionian sea. It was one of those afternoons you never forget, where the taste of food merges with your memory of the setting. It was what my husband calls "a day of pure Mediterranean bliss"—the sum of everything I've been writing about through the years, and which, when I recall it, always brings a smile to my face.

In the Ionians they replace the ham with thin rings of young red onions. In Italy they usually forgo any embellishment, preferring the simple combination of tomato and bread. One morning in Turkey, in the Euphrates Valley, where much of the Old Testament is set, I was handed a variation I call a "breakfast burrito." Turkish flat bread had been rolled around some smashed wood-charred onions and ripe tomato slathered with olive oil. The oil had been seasoned with a sprinkling of red pepper paste and dried mint.

I love these and other Mediterranean versions, but I adore the Catalan *pa amb tomàquet* the most. Perhaps this is because the first time I ate it—at a bar within La Boquería, the huge, boisterous, and legendary central market of Barcelona just off the Ramblas—was the first time I tasted it with jamón Ibérico. Jamón Ibérico is the extraordinary ham from the black-hoofed pigs raised on acorns around the town of Jabugo in the Extremadura region of Spain.

Alas, jamón Ibérico is not yet available in the United States. I know some importers who are working hard to bring it over. Hopefully, this will happen within the next few years. In the meantime, I sometimes add a very thin slice of serrano ham. But more often than not, I eat the bread and tomato alone.

Because this dish is so simple (a child can put it together in seconds), the ingredients must be perfect. Late summer vine-ripened tomatoes are a necessity. In northern California, where I live, we're blessed with wonderful multihued heirloom tomatoes from July through October. Off season, I look for sweet, juicy, aromatic cherry tomatoes, which I crush before spreading on the bread.

The bread is key. It should be country-style crusty and very fresh, preferably from a local bakery. When I'm at home, I always use bread from the Della Frattoria bakery in Sonoma County. I recommend grilling it the way the Catalans do, over a hardwood fire, or, if that's impossible, on a stovetop toaster grill set over a gas flame. This method is much preferred to the result obtainable from an electric toaster, in that the bread will be slightly charred by the flames.

Extra-virgin olive oil is one ingredient on which I never stint. I always buy the very best that I can find. If you choose a Tuscan oil, your *pa amb tomàquet* will be somewhat peppery; if you use a fine Spanish oil, it will be closer to the original. Either way works well for me, depending on my mood. As for salt, my favorite is the large-crystal British sea salt called Maldon, which dissolves when added to the crushed tomatoes.

Of course there are numerous "world class" dishes that I've written about and greatly enjoy—Spanish paella, Moroccan bisteeya, Provençal bouillabaisse, and cassoulet from southwest France. But when I'm going to eat alone, I always reach for that lovingly lettered yellow plate, the one that says *Pa amb Tomàquet*.

Pa amb Tomàquet

Cut a rustic-style bread with a serrated knife into ½-inch slices. Lightly toast the slices on a grill or in a toaster oven. Slather the toasted slices (on both sides) with freshly crushed ripe tomatoes. The layer must not be too thin or too thick—more like a thin, even red sheen. Sprinkle with fine salt. Slowly drizzle a light, golden extra-virgin olive oil on top on one side.

If you like, you can top the bread off with paper-thin slices of serrano ham or large, fat fillets of anchovy, preferably imported from l'Escale.

You may want to rub some garlic on the bread as well, but I've yet to meet a Catalan gastronome who would approve. Eat with a knife and fork.

The Lonely Palate

LAURA CALDER

Eight P.M. and stomachs all across the land are beginning to rumble. Down in the village, women are darting out to buy last-minute baguettes before the shutters on the *boulangerie* crash shut for the night. The men are drinking aperitifs of cold Chablis at the café-bar and chatting in duos and trios and quartets about why the village needs a new well. Any minute now, their coins will clink onto the counter. They'll wrap scarves around their necks and wander their separate ways through the wood-smoke-scented air, along cobblestone streets, in the final wisps of light, toward home. And there, waiting for them in the warm glow behind the windows, will be more talk and laughter, and no doubt an enormous pot of coq au vin or boeuf bourguignon or pot-au-feu, one of those mellow, classic, slowly cooked dishes, the privilege of families and intimate gatherings of loved ones.

Bastards.

Oh, come now! There's no need for this misery-loves-company nonsense. There's more than sour grapes in the kitchen for dinner, surely. I just have to make myself go in there and fix it. And then sit myself down and eat it. And, somehow, I must try to feel pleased about it.

It's rather odd: I have read quite a number of essays over the past few days on the subject of eating alone. You wouldn't believe for how many it ends up quasi-erotica. In one piece I read, the writer went so far as to take her dinner to the bathtub! Oh, the moans and groans of illicit pleasure, the unbridled indulgence that eating alone inspires in some!

I can remember one time eating alone and liking it, but it wasn't like that. It was at the end of my infantry-officer training (don't ask), and I had spent several months, obedient and sleep-deprived, being marched up and down in troops all over the place and eating two-year-old chicken cacciatore out of aluminum pouches, before crawling into trenches to be vigilant. The afternoon before the close of that lively period of my life, I was walking back to barracks and I passed a mess hall that we weren't allowed in, on pain of death. Through an open door, I spied a buffet table covered in tiny triangular sandwiches with no crusts. There was a tea urn at one end of it. I happened to be wearing webbing with a tin cup in the pouch. I pulled out the cup, held my breath, raced through the door, filled the cup with tea, grabbed a sandwich, tore out again, then stood panting around the corner under the eaves. Egg salad on Wonder bread has never been so tasty! Tea has never been so hot and sweet!

But that is the one and only time I can recall loving the fact that I was alone and eating at the same time. Otherwise, there is little I find more depressing, and frankly I do have a hard time believing anyone who tries to pass it off as anything else. If eating alone were truly the juicy experience some describe, there would be restaurants in the red-light districts full of plate-sized tables in curtained-off booths. Travelers would rave about the thrills of eating on airplanes, that peculiar form of solo dining, miraculously planned for a crowd, where everyone faces front like a brigade and nibbles silently off the world's only tables designed for one. On the other hand, since eating alone at least sometimes is a fact of life, I can understand wanting to make the best of it. And perhaps even exaggerating how good it all was, after the fact: it sometimes takes that in life to convince ourselves we've had fun.

"Like Lucullus!" you want to say. (He always gets dragged into this.) He was the Roman general famous for bellowing, "Tonight, Lucullus dines with Lucullus!" when his cook, having noticed that Lucullus had no guests and would therefore be dining alone, dared to serve him a less than feast-worthy meal. Well, not quite like Lucullus, although at least he had the good sense to stay home, rather than resort to a restaurant, where there's always the risk of being seated (in all one's lonesome splendor) in front of a mirror. Lucullus gets points for keeping up decorum. Fine. But don't forget, he had chefs in his kitchen fixing dinner for him, carrying it to his side, and lifting it onto his plate with a silver fork.* I'm sure that if Lucullus had had to cook for himself that night, like *moi*, he'd have been contemplating a boiled

---

*Okay, possibly there were no silver forks in ancient Rome, but I'm sure they'd have used some kind of elaborate, pricey pronged thing.

egg on the couch like the rest of us. (By the way, I say this after several weeks of dog-sitting in a grand empty house, where I've been subsisting on reheated pasta and store-bought cookies.)

These weeks remind me of that summer I spent in Spain a few years ago. I was staying all by myself in a borrowed house with no telephone, TV, or radio. It was just me, two gas burners, three months' worth of Booker Prize novels, and the grand idea that I was going to write a novel myself. By the end of the season, having eaten enough *pan con tomate* to soak up the entire Mediterranean Sea, I had grown Einsteinesque eyebrows (not ideas, alas!) and produced some of the most embarrassing writing of my lifetime. So that just goes to show you. Incidentally, not long afterward I found a quotation from Montaigne, which I now keep close at hand because it reminds me of where my priorities should be. To live, he said, "is the most illustrious of your occupations . . . to compose our character is our duty, not to compose books." I've found no better way of composing my character than by exposing it to other interesting characters, preferably over frequent lengthy dinners. (After all this time alone in the countryside, I can definitely feel my character going slack.)

This is not to say that I don't share the human need for solitude. On the contrary, I need more time alone than most people I know, but I really don't see why anyone would want to drag food into it. A book, yes. Walking shoes, perhaps. An inspiring view for an afternoon, sure. But a knife and a fork? You'd really have to be losing it. (Unless, of course, you're the Queen of England, just back from an official tour of the Commonwealth, in which case, yes, I can understand why you'd be just croaking for a plate of kippers mash in a lawn chair. But that's exceptional.)

Epicurus said that we should look for someone to eat and drink *with* before looking for something to eat and drink. I agree: for society's sake if not your own, never eat alone if you can avoid it. However, let's say you've exhausted the little black book, or, as is my case at the moment, you're six kilometers from the nearest house and you don't know who lives there anyway: then what?

I once knew a widow with a clever approach to the problem. When I was growing up, my mother visited a lot of old people and she'd drag me along to play little concerts for them on my violin. One of the ladies we occasionally called on, Ida Coffee, lived alone with a pump organ, a cat, and a dog, in a tiny gray wooden house with a red roof. We arrived one day, knocked several times, then finally stuck our heads in the door and called out. No Ida in sight. We were just turning to leave when she batted though the pantry door wearing an apron. "Come in!" she said. "I've just baked myself a birthday cake!" (The fact that she was turning ninety that day makes this all the more admirable.) We all sat around nibbling pieces of cake and drinking tea, after which I sawed out my virtuoso repertoire to mad applause: *Morning Has Broken, Devil's Dream, Edelweiss,* and little bits of Bach. Now, if only I had Ida's cook-and-the-company-will-come philosophy bred in my bones! Ach, but I don't. There's no point going to great strides to concoct something spectacular for myself, because I simply won't appreciate it on my own. On the other hand, if I wash down that bag of cashews on the counter with a glass of wine and call it dinner, I'm going to feel as though I belong living under a bridge.

Perhaps there's a solution that strikes a middle ground, and before I send my immune system crashing to an all-time low, I'd better march myself straight into the kitchen and adopt it: one-bowl suppers, from scratch. Here's my reasoning: If it's possible to eat whatever has been made out of one bowl, chances are it will also have been possible to cook it in one pot, which is convenient. Eating out of a bowl requires only one utensil, so with bowl in one hand, and fork or spoon in the other, I can chew away at a meditative pace in a cozy armchair, rather than behind the candelabra at the far end of a table for twelve, like the last living member of a fallen dynasty. And bowls are comforting vessels. There's something admirably self-sufficient about them. They seem specifically designed to hold the kind of simple, trusty fare that, although it probably won't inspire lust, at least will help satisfy a lonely kind of hunger . . .

. . . Nice try. That would have been an ideal ending to this saga if weren't for the fact that, instead of cooking, I just went over and did in all those cashews. (Rats!) Let's face it: the truth about eating alone, despite our best intentions, is that nine times out of ten we eat badly. We eat inadequate food; we eat it too fast; and we eat it slouched over a computer or sprawled in front of a television, with all the enlightened social skills of seagulls. I'm convinced that this affects the way we live our lives afterward. It's no doubt why I've been scuffing around in worn-out slippers and a slouchy turtleneck for days, avoiding the future. (It's probably why the whole world seems to be falling apart at the seams.) Eating alone is not nature's way. Babies never eat alone. They can't. Children don't, unless they're in tragic circumstances. Old people eat alone regularly and it's dreadful. No wonder they lose their appetites. My theory (and I have several solo dinners behind me to back it up) is that to compose a happy character, and thus contribute to making the world a nice place to live in, you've either got *to be fed* (that is, by someone *other than yourself* who cares about you), which feels good and means that you're part of something larger than yourself; or, you've got *to be the person feeding* (that is, *other* people—not just dogs!—that *you* care about). That has the same positive effect.

Luckily, I have both to look forward to next week, when I finally get out of here. For now, however, I guess the best I can do is pretend that those cashews were just an aperitif. And, while I'm at it, I might as well make out that I'm just back from an exhausting tour of the Commonwealth.

Kippers Mash

Ideal quiet one-bowl comfort food for one. (Although I'd rather it were for two.)

> Potatoes
> Butter
> Milk
> Salt and pepper
> Tinned kippers, drained
> Parsley (optional)

Peel and boil potatoes until very tender. Drain. Mash them up with generous quantities of butter, milk, salt, and pepper. Mash in a drained tin of kippers. Scoop into a bowl and eat. No parsley required, but it never hurts, either.

How to Cook in a
New York Apartment
LAURA DAVE

Whatever you do, on your first night in the new apartment, do not cook salmon. The fish smell will move in, like an unwelcome roommate. When you return from your first day of your new bad job, it will be there to greet you—hovering in your still unopened boxes, your sofa, your new walls.

You won't understand. In the old converted schoolhouse far out in the country, you cooked this dish all the time—broiled salmon and rich butter sauce, sautéed broccoli and herbs—the tall kitchen windows letting the smells out as soon as they entered.

But things are different now. You don't have a life-size kitchen anymore; you don't have big, hopeful windows; you don't even have a room for your bed. That whole first week, you will lie on the far side of your bed.

On the far side of the freezer, the rest of the salmon.

. . .

There are rules for cooking for yourself in a New York apartment:

1. **Don't cook that which leaves its smell behind.**
   Think not only of the salmon, but of garlic—
   its small, slippery madness—of Cuban food,
   which makes you sick anyway, of soft, round
   cheeses.
2. **Don't prepare what doesn't keep easily.** Your
   freezer is the size and the width of a pencil
   case.
3. **Do involve peanut butter whenever possible.**
   A jar will run you $3.99—a bargain in this
   city!—and can be used for everything from
   peanut butter pie to the world's easiest pad
   Thai sauce: ½ cup of peanut butter, 2 tablespoons of vegetable oil, brown sugar, soy
   sauce, red pepper flakes to taste.

You need music to cook to, especially under less-than-ideal conditions. Break it out. Joni Mitchell and Bob Dylan for soups.
Bruce Springsteen for stews. Turn up "Atlantic City" when you're
making beef stroganoff. (Forget the package of onion soup mix.
Cut fresh onions, let them simmer in ⅓ cup of olive oil, ½ cup of
water; one chopped portobello mushroom.) The heat coming
from the stovetop is making you flushed. To find balance, cover
your radiator with the red beach towel that has survived six apart-

ment moves. Pour yourself a second glass of wine. Hum along.
*Put your makeup on, fix your hair up pretty, and meet me tonight in
Atlantic City.*

Stop humming.

Remember.

Nobody cooks in Manhattan. But don't let this discourage
you. Many people don't do anything here but stumble and race
and hope, waiting for their real lives to begin. There is the neighbor to your left, who moved into her small studio just until she
got married. She is sixty-seven. There is the one to your right
still trying to finish a documentary about the making of *Star
Wars*. They are good people. Smile at them in the hallway. Leave
them fresh coffee. Remind yourself that you are back here to do
something hard—go to medical school, write a novel, become a
clown. It's really something closer to the second, but you like to
pretend it's the third. You like to pretend it's becoming a clown.
The circus, after all, scared the crap out of you growing up, the
same way not ever managing to finish this manuscript scares the
crap out of you now.

Buy yourself books named things like *Quit Clowning Around*!
Buy yourself a red nose.

Smile, all the time.

Avoid thoughts of the boyfriends and half-boyfriends you
cooked for in the various cities and half-cities where you found
them. (London liked seared tuna and wasabi green beans; L.A.

liked roasted chicken stuffed with lemon; and New England—
how cold it got in New England!—liked your father's French
toast: challah bread soaked in butter and two teaspoons of
vanilla, sliced peaches on top.)

Think instead of your great Southern mother—whose smallest meals involved three courses and clean white china—and
who taught you that cooking is something you do for others:
cooking and caretaking, all locked up, one simple promise. Add
this to the list of things you blame her for.

To cook for yourself—beyond a plate of macaroni and cheese,
beyond heated-up beans—feels like an impossible luxury. Tell
yourself whatever you need to tell yourself to do it anyway: it will
save you money and time (the right dish can last you several dinners and a long, good lunch). It will save you. Don't think too
much about the rest of it—the part that cooking for yourself
represents—that you matter, even when no one is watching. That
you have never, before now, thought to cook for yourself, thought
to be there for yourself in so many ways you naturally have been
there for everyone else. Make a grocery list instead. Head to the
store. Stock up on tinfoil. And before you know it, you have
stopped thinking and started doing. Which, as you are starting to
figure out, is the first step to making anything become real.

The dish you've chosen is chicken Parmigiana. This is a dish that
is hard to do badly. But there is a world of difference between
doing it not badly and doing it right.

First, there are the homemade sauces: one for the chicken, a lighter one for the accompanying pasta. Start with the chicken's sauce: plum tomatoes and fresh oregano, onions, grated pecorino cheese. Let simmer on low heat. Blend olive oil, roasted tomatoes, and basil in a bowl. The pasta sauce is ready. Bread the meat in eggs and milk and crumbs. If you are feeling frisky, add a little coconut extract.

You are barefoot now. You are wearing a long summer dress. And the countertops—once bare themselves—are covered with vegetable leaves and peppermint sticks, fancy oil bottles and broken pieces of baguette. Understand, if only in a distant way, that this is not a mess.

Take the chicken from the oven and rest it on the stovetop to cool. Lick your thumb. Then lie down on the couch to rest yourself, if only for a minute, wrapping your dress around you like a blanket. You don't plan to fall asleep there. As you do, though—fall asleep—reflect briefly that we rarely plan to do the things that most need to happen.

When you wake up, it is three in the morning. You close the window, pad over to the fridge. Wrap up the chicken and wrap up the pasta, placing them neatly together in a soft blue container. Rest it on the fridge shelf, under that soft blue light. Close the refrigerator. You are too tired right now to give the dish its proper due.

So you save it. For tomorrow.

Let's talk about tomorrow.

How well it goes. Something good happens at work—

something really good happens. The details don't matter. (Even clowning is pretty boring to the nonclown.) What matters is the feeling. And the feeling is like the first time you blew a bubblegum bubble, or made noise when you whistled. It's like the first time you heard the Clash.

Suddenly, anything is possible.

And so you call your oldest friend, a botanist, to help you celebrate (botanists know how to party, after all), and the two of you head to a nearby bar to drink mint juleps and watch the Kentucky Derby. Or: maybe it is too beautiful to be inside and the two of you head up the Aqueduct trail for a celebratory bike ride.

The point is: you fall down. Hard. (Both bars and bikes precipitate this in you.) You fall, the spokes in the bike catching at your ankle. And when you look up, you see him, just standing there. He has bright blue eyes that match, a little freakishly, his bright blue bike. He also has the nicest smile you've ever seen, which he shines right at you. And it's the weirdest thing because in all the cities and half-cities where you've found boys, you've never had the feeling that you have now. You can't do anything wrong.

The following thought will flash through your mind, briefly, before you lose it forever: it's related. The great work victory and this nice meeting with a blue-eyed person *have to be* related to the many hours you spent cooking the day before. All for yourself. How could it not be? You are wearing it on your face, like a badge. (Literally on your face. You raced out of the house, a little piece of tomato on the side of your cheek, a little piece in your hair.)

"Are you okay?" he asks.

"I think I am," you say, brushing yourself off. Smiling back at him.

In the background, your botanist friend eats a leaf.

Eleven P.M. The silliest and best time to eat by yourself.

All the windows in your New York apartment are open. Your stereo is tuned to country music. You are cuddled on the couch in your thick white socks with your soft blue bowl of chicken Parmigiana.

This is when the phone rings. This is the most important part.

You don't answer it. Even though it may be the blue-eyed person. Even though it may be something about work. Even though it may be flowers or promises ready to be kept or the hope of an easier tomorrow. (It does turn out, in a way you couldn't have prepared for, that tomorrow will get easier. That there is good news on the other end of that phone. That your dreams, if not coming true, are coming closer.)

But know this. Even if someone tells you it is corny later. Even if someone tells you that it is a coincidence. Good things happen, because right then, when you need to most, you sit still. You sit still in your seat—Willie Nelson and Loretta Lynn duet-ing in the background; the fast May heat swimming around you. And for you—for nobody else—you take a first, great bite.

Potatoes and Love: Some Reflections
NORA EPHRON

THE BEGINNING

I have friends who begin with pasta, and friends who begin with rice, but whenever I fall in love, I begin with potatoes. Sometimes meat and potatoes and sometimes fish and potatoes, but always potatoes. I have made a lot of mistakes falling in love, and regretted most of them, but never the potatoes that went with them.

Not just any potato will do when it comes to love. There are people who go on about the virtues of plain potatoes—plain boiled new potatoes with a little parsley or dill, or plain baked potatoes with crackling skins—but my own feeling is that a taste for plain potatoes coincides with cultural antecedents I do not possess, and that in any case, the time for plain potatoes—if there is ever a time for plain potatoes—is never at the beginning of something. It is also, I should add, never at the end of something. Perhaps you can get away with plain potatoes in the middle, although I have never been able to.

All right, then: I am talking about crisp potatoes. Crisp potatoes require an immense amount of labor. It's not just the peeling, which is one of the few kitchen chores no electric device has been invented to alleviate; it's also that the potatoes, once peeled, must be cut into whatever shape you intend them to be, put into water to be systematically prevented from turning a loathsome shade of bluish-brownish-black, and then meticulously dried to ensure that they crisp properly. All this takes time, and time, as any fool can tell you, is what true romance is about. In fact, one of the main reasons why you must make crisp potatoes in the beginning is that if you don't make them in the beginning, you never will. I'm sorry to be so cynical about this, but that's the truth.

There are two kinds of crisp potatoes that I prefer above all others. The first are called Swiss potatoes, and they're essentially a large potato pancake of perfect hash browns; the flipping of the pancake is so wildly dramatic that the potatoes themselves are almost beside the point. The second are called potatoes Anna; they are thin circles of potato cooked in a shallow pan in the oven and then turned onto a plate in a darling mound of crunchy brownness. Potatoes Anna is a classic French recipe, but there is something so homely and old-fashioned about them that they can usually be passed off as either an ancient family recipe or something you just made up.

For Swiss potatoes: Peel 3 large (or 4 small) russet potatoes (or all-purpose if you can't get russets) and put them in cold water to cover. Start 4 tablespoons butter and 1 tablespoon cooking oil melting in a nice heavy large frying pan. Working quickly, dry the potatoes and grate them on the grating disk of the Cuisinart. Put them into a colander and squeeze out as much water as you can. Then dry them again on paper towels. You will need more paper towels to do this than you ever thought possible. Dump the potatoes into the frying pan, patting them down with a spatula, and cook over medium heat for about 15 minutes, until the bottom of the pancake is brown. Then, while someone is watching, loosen the pancake and, with one incredibly deft motion, flip it over. Salt it generously. Cook 5 minutes more. Serves two.

For potatoes Anna: Peel 3 large (or 4 small) russet potatoes (or Idahos if you can't get russets) and put them in water. Working quickly, dry each potato and slice into 1/16-inch rounds. Dry them with paper towels, round by round. Put 1 tablespoon clarified butter into a cast-iron skillet and line the skillet with overlapping potatoes. Dribble clarified butter and salt and pepper over them. Repeat twice. Put into a 425° oven for 45 minutes, pressing the potatoes down now and then. Then turn up the oven to 500° and cook 10 more minutes. Flip onto a round platter. Serves two.

THE MIDDLE (I)

One day the inevitable happens. I go to the potato drawer to make potatoes and discover that the little brown buggers I bought in a large sack a few weeks earlier have gotten soft and mushy and are sprouting long and quite uninteresting vines. In addition, one of them seems to have developed an odd brown leak, and the odd brown leak appears to be the cause of a terrible odor that in only a few seconds has permeated the entire kitchen. I throw out the potatoes and look in the cupboard for a box of pasta. This is the moment when the beginning ends and the middle begins.

THE MIDDLE (II)

Sometimes, when a loved one announces that he has decided to go on a low-carbohydrate, low-fat, low-salt diet (thus ruling out the possibility of potatoes, should you have been so inclined), he is signaling that the middle is ending and the end is beginning.

THE END

In the end, I always want potatoes. Mashed potatoes. Nothing like mashed potatoes when you're feeling blue. Nothing like getting into bed with a bowl of hot mashed potatoes already loaded with butter, and methodically adding a thin cold slice of butter to every forkful. The problem with mashed potatoes, though, is that they require almost as much hard work as crisp potatoes, and when you're feeling blue the last thing you feel like is hard work. Of course, you can always get someone to make the mashed potatoes for you, but let's face it: the reason you're blue is that there *isn't* anyone to make them for you. As a result, most people do not have nearly enough mashed potatoes in their lives, and when they do, it's almost always at the wrong time.

(You can, of course, train children to mash potatoes, but you should know that Richard Nixon spent most of his childhood making mashed potatoes for his mother and was extremely methodical about getting the lumps out. A few lumps make mashed potatoes more authentic, if you ask me, but that's not the point. The point is that perhaps children should not be trained to mash potatoes.)

For mashed potatoes: Put 1 large (or 2 small) potatoes in a large pot of salted water and bring to a boil. Lower the heat and simmer for at least 20 minutes, until tender. Drain and place the potatoes back in the pot and shake over low heat to eliminate excess moisture. Peel. Put through a potato ricer and immediately add 1 tablespoon heavy cream and as much melted butter and salt and pepper as you feel like. Eat immediately. Serves one.

Instant Noodles

RATTAWUT LAPCHAROENSAP

The Ethiopians were dying. They were on television all the time—their dirty faces, their sunken cheeks, their bloated stomachs, their abstracted, fly-orbited eyes. Help was needed; something had to be done. So various governments sent food, medicine, supplies, doctors, nurses, etc. So pop stars gathered to raise money by singing rock ballads. *We are the world,* the pop stars crooned, swaying in unison. *We are the children. Let them know it's Christmas.*

Meanwhile, in the schoolyards of Bangkok, "Ethiopian" became an epithet for skinny children with large, outsized heads like me. *Hey Ethiopian,* the other seven-year-olds would catcall, sniggering. *Yeah, you. With the glasses and the gangly arms. With the big head. With the dark, shitty skin. That's right. We're talking to you. You mouth breather. You fucking Ethiopian.*

I didn't mind. At least they didn't call me Chinese or Cambodian or Muslim or—worst of all—Laotian. "Laotian" implied that you were ugly, poor, unfashionable, stupid. No one would talk to you. You'd sit silently by the garbage bins during lunch with the other Laotians, wallowing in the shame of your communal Laotianness. The roaches and mice would scuttle around your shoes, and everything you ate would smell like wet trash.

And so I sat alone each day eating instant noodles, which I bought for two baht and fifty satang from a vendor who was probably an actual Laotian immigrant. She didn't speak much Thai, and when she did she spoke with a lilting accent. She always prepared my lunch in less than ten seconds—a bowl, a brick of dried noodles, a ladle of boiling broth—and I would go to my corner of the canteen to mark time with each spoonful.

It is a stock scenario, the abject child eating alone at school, lifeblood of so many sitcoms and young-adult novels. The image's ubiquity must have something to do with the school canteen's special status as a primal site of unchecked peer sociality. And so the maligned child fulfills, with each bitter mouthful, her circular, uninvited destiny: she eats alone because she is abject and she is abject because she eats alone. But the tragedy is not eating alone as such—it's the transformation of the very meaning of eating itself, from a nourishing, comforting, and familial activity to one that is cold, pathological, and solipsistic.

But there are, of course, worse things than eating alone at a public elementary school in Bangkok. For one, I could've been an actual Ethiopian.

The Thai government—not to be outdone by its colleagues, let alone its colleagues' pop stars—decided to make a contribution to the relief effort in Ethiopia. They solicited nonperishable food items from citizens and businesses alike, and soon received a sizable donation from an instant noodle company. Several planeloads of instant noodles were sent to Addis Ababa as a gesture of the Thai people's goodwill. Upon arrival, however, the planes were sent back with their cargo—aid agencies had found the noodles to be wholly lacking in nutritional value.

Get this stuff out of here, the aid agencies are reported to have said. *They'll only exacerbate the crisis. Instant noodles are bad for you.*

At least that's the cautionary tale told to many Thai children when instant noodles flooded the markets in the early eighties. Alarmingly cheap, colorfully packaged, and offered in an impossibly wide variety of flavors and noodle sizes, the offending foodstuff was also rumored, at one point, to contain powdered marijuana in its seasoning packages. This was said to account for its strangely addictive quality, and I remember sneaking several Mama-brand chicken-flavored seasoning packages into my bedroom as a seven-year-old, believing I was embarking on an inaugural experiment with illicit drugs. I nearly sucked at the foil to get at every grain, and then I lay back on my bed and waited for magic to happen.

No magic happened. I didn't get high, just really thirsty.

Around the time of this failed experiment, a friend showed me a trick. This consisted of crushing a sealed bag of instant noodles, opening it, fishing out the seasoning pack, and pouring the seasoning back onto the noodles. He shook the bag for a few seconds before offering me the mixture.

Potato chips, he declared, smiling proudly.

Thai *potato chips,* he continued, when I just blinked at him. *Half as cheap and twice as tasty as the* farang *variety.*

I didn't realize it at the time, but my friend had taught me how to prepare my first meal, and he had also taught me something about thriftiness and ingenuity and cross-cultural mimesis. But more important—as I said to him at the time, sprinkling a handful into my mouth—it was fucking delicious. Those Ethiopians didn't know what they were missing.

My mother taught me how to prepare a bowl of instant noodles on the stove. It was the first thing I ever learned to cook and remains, to this day, one of the few things I cook when I'm alone.

Bamee *idiot,* she said as we waited in the kitchen for the water to boil. Idiot noodles. Meaning: even an idiot could prepare a decent bowl, though she couldn't resist adding that it also meant if I ate too many, too often, I might run the risk of retardation.

This stuff is bad for you, she proclaimed.

But you can make it good, she continued. *It's what you add to it that counts.*

We added Chinese cabbage, green beans, spring onions, and sliced hot dogs into the pot that afternoon. Near the end, as the noodles softened, she showed me how to separate an egg's white from its yolk, dribbling the translucent substance into the pot by transferring the yolk back and forth between its broken shells. Strings of egg white puffed and brightened upon contact with the boiling broth. Then she placed the yolk into the bottom of our serving bowl—the heat from the broth, she said, would be sufficient to cook it.

The dish hardly resembled the meal I'd been consuming at school. While my lunches had consisted of nothing but noodles and broth, my bowl now teemed with other ingredients; while the vendor at school had taken less than ten seconds, my mother had taken nearly ten minutes; and while I ate my noodles at school alone, disconsolately spooning each mouthful, I now sat with my mother and my sister on either side, chatting between bites about nothing in particular.

I moved to Ithaca, New York, in 1996 to attend Cornell University. It was the first time I had ever lived alone.

One afternoon, I came across a Chinese grocery on Route 13 that stocked a decent selection of Mama, Yumyum, and Waiwai instant noodles. I nearly wept at the sight of them in their bright and shiny packages, lined up neatly beside their Korean, Chinese, and Japanese counterparts. I had tried several American brands of instant noodles since arriving from Bangkok but found them all inadequate—the broth flavoring had always seemed rather *too* artificial, the noodles texturally suspicious. Here, then, were my madeleines—material links to a former life—and I remember gathering several packages into my arms as if they were children that I had lost.

But instant noodles were not simply an item of homesick nostalgia. They were also—at two dollars a dozen—economically viable. Shortly after I arrived in Ithaca, the baht was devalued, the Thai economy subsequently crashed, and my mother informed me that the length of my American adventure depended upon my ability to pay my own way. I watched as scholarships ran dry, middle-class fortunes crumbled, and several Thai students headed home without the degrees they'd hoped for. Very little was left of the already negligible Thai community in Ithaca. It was the loneliest time of my life.[1]

All new immigrants yearn periodically for familiar foods. The fulfillment of that yearning can be a difficult, if not impossible, proposition. Ingredients are often scarce. Resources are often limited. And restaurants offering one's native cuisine tend to serve inadequate approximations of beloved dishes (at unheard-of prices, to boot). The gap between the memory of a good meal and the attempt to re-create it in a foreign country—to make oneself feel, in a sense, more at home—can reinforce rather than eradicate feelings of dislocation and homesickness. This would be the case, I suspect, even if one managed to re-create a dish in all its subtle, "authentic" aspects, for there are things that one can never re-create on a stove. Because of this ambivalence, immigrants know—perhaps more than most—that though eating can make you full, it can also often feel like fasting.

The instant noodles that I ate alone in Ithaca might have been identical to the instant noodles of my childhood, but the taste, so to speak, was entirely different. The reasons for this, of course, were obvious. My mother was not there. My sister was

---

1. Nevertheless, I don't want to overemphasize the degree of my poverty at the time, for I often find inappropriate those who conflate the temporary deprivations of student living with the long-term despair inflicted by intractable economic disadvantage. More often than not—particularly at institutions like Cornell—those who would claim the mantle of poverty tend to have trust funds and ample salaries awaiting them as soon as they leave. Poverty figures as a romantic rite of passage rather than a cruel fate doled out by a cruel world, and it's always struck me as a mark of true privilege when one can dabble in the darkness of economic despair—eating instant noodles in one's dorm room only to go back to one's suburban house during vacations to feast like a rarefied gourmand.

not there. The students who called me Ethiopian were not there. The Laotian vendor was not there. My friend who taught me how to make Thai potato chips was not there. I was alone, in a half-basement studio in a small New York town, thousands of miles from the people I loved, people I would not see again for many years. I was cold and I was exhausted: frat boys woke me with their whooping at night, emptied their beer-filled bladders against my window, and occasionally, when I walked down the street, American children taunted me with what I can only describe as fake Chinese. No matter how fastidiously I followed my mother's recipe for instant noodles, these were entirely different noodles, and I knew that I would need to learn, with time, to find comfort in their flavors, lest I resign myself to bitterness.

Food Nomad

ROSA JURJEVICS

I have never been a conventional eater and, considering my lineage, it's no wonder. My mother, the writer Laurie Colwin, was a foodie with a salt tooth. She was pan-national in her tastes—she never met a culture whose cooking she flat-out disliked. She brought home Chinese herbs, Ethiopian bread, Jamaican desserts, and Mexican salsa. She mixed condiments based on Indian recipes and tried her hand at traditional English puddings, the failed latter of which got her into comical culinary trouble at a dinner party once. In short, she was not just a consumer but a fierce emulator, often employing extraordinary measures to obtain her recipes. She was known for traipsing downtown and up, unafraid to pick up a bun, a bread, a cheese and ask "What's in this?" I remember her in the kitchen, worrying over a stove full of boiling pots, the counter littered with various utensils, stirring vigorously with the sleeves of her sweater rolled up past her elbows. Several hours and cross-continental phone calls later, she would more often than not emerge victorious, hot bowl or plate or tureen in hand.

My father, the publisher Juris Jurjevics, is not a cook except by necessity, yet he has his own set of food-related habits. Both a European and a Vietnam War veteran, he is content to consume his meals directly from cans, bags, and packets. Growing up, I would sit beside him on his bed and listen to daytime talk radio while we shared Goya chickpeas and pickled cabbage, lentils and black beans, packages of M&Ms and toasted almonds. Veterans Day meant Spam and Vienna sausages, served as is save for frilly toothpicks stabbed into their centers. Our Saturday breakfasts were crêpelike pancakes native to Latvia, his homeland, and sick food was a stockpot of slow-boiled cabbage soup. His love for root vegetables—the food of his people, as he's known to say— and my mother's affinity for kitchen adventures filled our plates with parsnips, beets, carrots, and potatoes. My grandmother's baking provided us with saffron cakes and peppery ginger cookies throughout the holiday season.

These days, as a grown-up responsible for feeding myself, I realize more than ever just how much I have inherited my parents' eating habits. There are times I have opened my fridge and grinned to see, next to my roommates' tubs of peanut butter and mayonnaise, my little jar of capers, a staple in my fridge at home but an anomaly here, or a packet of rice bean cakes in the freezer beside the Chubby Hubby ice cream. Like my mother, I often crave sour, turning to cornichons strong enough to hurt the taste buds, or freshly peeled organic lemons. Sometimes it's salt I want, and I go on ravenous sprees, buying long slices of lox and tins of black olives, sautéing zucchini and chicken in oil and garlic salt. And I am just as much my father. When I return home for holidays and observe him, hunkered over his manuscripts as he eats from a jar of nuts, I realize I have copied him movement for movement as I nosh and study. Film theory books in front of me, I pluck hearts of palm spears from their cans, spoon up cold beans, or dip my fingers absently into a tub of shredded red cabbage—his favorite. I have, as every child fears, turned into my parents. And I love it.

My friends, however, have not always shared my enthusiasm. At one former apartment, a four-flight Boston walk-up, I tried to tempt them with Latvian pancakes, goat-milk yogurt, and my favorite Chinese candy, a dried sugar-and-salt preserved plum known as *wamoi*. They either politely declined or recoiled in horror, depending. This was nothing new for me; in grade school, I was known as the girl with the weirdest lunch, coming in with homemade multigrain bread and all-natural treats bearing disarmingly accurate names like "fruit leather." I tried and tried to trade; nobody bit. In Boston, I am left to enjoy my Japanese seaweed snacks and tomato-paste sandwiches solo. Oh, well. More for me.

If my mother was a food pioneer and my father is a food appreciator, I am a food nomad. My favorite thing to do on a gray, rainy day is to go deep into Boston's Chinatown—imagine the population of New York's condensed into less than half the square footage—and seek out my favorite pan-Asian treats. It is during the pre-midterm, calm-before-the-storm week that I venture out into the drizzle, sans umbrella, on a search for something more than the compulsory pizza and pasta that comprise the American college diet. Chinatown is still busy, tired faces under the coming rain. I pass an adult movie house and a smoke shop and finally duck into a narrow side street bordered by dark, postindustrial buildings. And there it is, sandwiched between a seedy video store and a greasy-windowed restaurant—my favorite sublevel market, nameless, fluorescent-lit, and beckoning.

The market is a wonder, an Asian Balducci's of sorts. It is usually busy, filled with families and solitary older women who stoop over their carts and chatter impatiently at the annoyed stock clerks. The front of the market is dominated by freezer bins containing frozen buns, entire dim sum meals (in the style of Lean Cuisine), and packets of poultry parts I dare not guess the names for. Fruit abounds: oversized apples, bulging grapefruits, longan in a bucket, and, of course, the spiky, craggy, and foul-smelling durian. Vegetables have their own wall toward the back. Bok choy bottoms gleam in the white light, leeks and celery are stacked stalk by stalk, tofu floats in water. Adjacent to the produce is the seafood counter, next to which sits a bank of Plexiglas fish tanks containing discontented-looking creatures that, next to all the bright packaging, seem vaguely prehistoric. They swim in their holding cells while their felled brethren lie belly up on beds of ice beside them.

I am the only white face in the market and, feeling vaguely like a tourist, I cruise the isles with my basket, passing cans and boxes and vacuum-sealed packets of things I have never seen, the names of which I cannot read. The labels of soups and mixes feature photos and shoddy English. Candy labels boast rosy-cheeked children with eyes closed in delighted laughter. Here I make my selections: lychee nuts in syrup, pearl mushrooms, udon noodles, the dreaded *wamoi*. I wander past the housewares section, turning over soup spoons and Buddha statues, sniffing incense, poking snow globes.

As a kid, I used to take these trips with my parents. My mother and I would set out for Chinatown to get dim sum or venture off to the Little India section of New York for fiery-red tandoori chicken and yogurt lassi drinks. We'd hit the Union Square farmers' market in the crisp fall air and select apples from wooden boxes and sample twice-baked dark pretzels. With Dad, it was a different kind of exotic: we ate the forbidden foods my mother loathed and banned from the house. At his office, we drank deliciously foul strawberry-milk beverages and ate from little white bags of marshmallow twists, giggling, at his desk. On the Roosevelt Island tram, we ate glazed doughnuts and Mc-Donald's fries high above the East River, landing for a stop at the candy store for sour straws and Cokes.

Heaping my basket at the market, as much a delighted stranger here as I was in the adventure spots of my childhood, I think of them both. Roti and cabbage. Lemons and lentils. Goat cheese and pancakes. Mom and Dad.

The lady at the checkout counter gives me the once-over, takes my money without a word, and hands over my bright pink bags. I stuff them in my backpack and make my way home, up the four flights to my apartment. My roommates, watching television, studying, and lounging, look up.

"Whatcha got?" they ask me, pointing to the bags.

I look down at the tops of the cans, at the package of *wamoi* peeking up at me. My roommates crane their necks to see into the bags, hoping for cookies, cheese, packaged bread, the staples of our hodgepodge household. For a moment my choices seem strange, even to me, a blend of foods no normal person would put together. I consider what to say and toy with the plastic edge of the *wamoi*'s shrinkwrap, still half heavy with memories. I look back at my roommates; my bags are full but to them they are empty, the contents inedible. My treats and childhood favorites hold no context for them, no afternoon sojourns with Mom, no watching Dad twist the can opener in his trademark pajamas. So I shrug and head for the kitchen.

"Nothing," I reply. "Just food."

Contributors

EDITOR

Jenni Ferrari-Adler is a graduate of Oberlin College and the University of Michigan, where she received an MFA in fiction. She has worked as a reader for *The Paris Review,* a bookseller, an egg seller, and an assistant at a literary agency. Her short fiction has been published in numerous magazines. She lives in New York City.

CONTRIBUTORS

Steve Almond lives and grills in Arlington, Massachusetts. He writes about a variety of oral pleasures, most notably in his story collections, *My Life in Heavy Metal* and *The Evil B.B. Chow.*

Jonathan Ames is the author of the novels *I Pass Like Night, The Extra Man,* and *Wake Up, Sir!;* the essay collections *What's Not to Love?, My Less Than Secret Life,* and *I Love You More Than You Know;* and the editor of *Sexual Metamorphosis: An Anthology of Transsexual Memoirs.* Ames performs frequently as a storyteller and comedian, and has been a recurring guest on *The Late Show with David Letterman.*

Jami Attenberg is the author of *Instant Love* and *The Kept Man* (forthcoming). She has written for *Salon, Print, Nylon, Nerve,* and the *San Francisco Chronicle,* among other publications. She lives in Brooklyn.

Laura Calder is the author of *French Food at Home.* Her writing has appeared in publications including *Vogue Entertaining & Travel, Gourmet, Gastronomica, Salon, The Times* (London), the *Los Angeles Times, The Wine Journal,* and *Flare* magazine. Her first television series, *French Food at Home,* will air in 2007.

Mary Cantwell was the author of three memoirs: *American Girl, Speaking with Strangers,* and *Manhattan, When I Was Young.* She was an editor at *Mademoiselle* and *Vogue* and a member of the editorial board of the *New York Times.*

Dan Chaon is the author of *You Remind Me of Me, Fitting Ends,* and *Among the Missing,* which was a finalist for the National Book Award. His work has received many honors, most recently the Literature Prize from the American Academy of Arts and Letters. He lives in Cleveland, where he does all the cooking for his wife and sons.

Laurie Colwin was the author of five novels: *Happy All the Time; Family Happiness; Goodbye without Leaving; Shine On, Bright and*

Dangerous Object; A Big Storm Knocked It Over; three collections of short stories: *Passion and Affect, Another Marvelous Thing, The Lone Pilgrim;* and two collections of essays: *Home Cooking* and *More Home Cooking.*

Laura Dave was born in New York City, where she currently resides. She is the author of *London Is the Best City in America,* which is currently being developed as a feature film at Universal Studios. She is at work on her second novel and a screenplay.

Courtney Eldridge is the author of *Unkempt,* a collection of short stories. Her work has appeared in numerous publications, including *A Public Space, McSweeney's,* and the *Mississippi Review.* She lives in New York City and is working on her first novel.

Nora Ephron is a journalist, novelist, playwright, screenwriter, and director. Her credits include *Heartburn, When Harry Met Sally, Sleepless in Seattle, You've Got Mail,* and *Imaginary Friends.* Her latest book is *I Feel Bad About My Neck: And Other Thoughts on Being a Woman.* She lives in New York City.

Erin Ergenbright is a codirector of the Loggernaut Reading Series and the author of *The Ex-Boyfriend Cookbook* (with Thisbe Nissen). Her work has appeared in *Tin House, The Believer, Indiana Review, The May Queen: Women on Life, Love, Work, and Pulling It All Together in Your 30s,* and elsewhere. She teaches writing workshops in the greater Portland area and is frequently preoccupied by the idea of owning a horse.

M. F. K. Fisher was the author of numerous books of essays and reminiscences, many of which have become American classics.

Colin Harrison is the author of the novels *Afterburn, Break and Enter, Bodies Electric, The Havana Room,* and *Manhattan Nocturne.* He and his wife, Kathryn Harrison, live in Brooklyn.

Marcella Hazan, the acknowledged godmother of Italian cooking in America, has written six cookbooks, including *The Classic Italian Cookbook, Essentials of Italian Cooking,* and *Marcella Cucina.* She lives with her husband, Victor, himself an authority on Italian food and wine, in Longboat Key, Florida.

Amanda Hesser is the food editor at *The New York Times Magazine.* She writes two columns—"The Way We Eat" and "The Arsenal"—in the weekly magazine and edits the *Times'*s food magazine, *T: Living.* She has published two books, *The Cook and the Gardener* and *Cooking for Mr. Latte,* both of which won the International Association of Culinary Professionals' Literary Food Writing award. Her next book is a collection of *New York Times* recipes from 1853 until today.

Holly Hughes is the editor of the annual *Best Food Writing* anthology, and the author of *Frommer's New York City with Kids* and *Frommer's 500 Places to Take Your Kids Before They Grow Up.* She lives in New York City and has three children, all of whom know how to cook.

Jeremy Jackson was raised in central Missouri and is a graduate of Vassar College and the Iowa Writers' Workshop, where he received a teaching-writing fellowship. He's the author of the novels *In Summer* and *Life at These Speeds*, which is being developed for a feature film. His cookbooks include *Desserts That Have Killed Better Men Than Me*, *Good Day for a Picnic*, and *The Cornbread Book*, which was nominated for a James Beard Award. He has written about food for the *Chicago Tribune* and *The Washington Post*, and was featured in *Food & Wine* magazine. He lives in Iowa City, Iowa.

Rosa Jurjevics is, among other things, a video editor and writer. When not doodling on napkins, she spends her time animating, meeting deadlines, and wrangling computer files. Her written work has been featured in the *San Diego Reader* and *Real Simple* magazine and her 2001 video, *Heirographics*, was chosen for the HBO *30x30 Kid Flicks* film festival. Her art has been featured in various shows organized by the SunArts Collective in New York.

Ben Karlin was the head writer, then the executive producer, of *The Daily Show with Jon Stewart* from 1999 to 2006. In 2005 he cocreated *The Colbert Report*, starring Stephen Colbert. Karlin collaborated with Jon Stewart, David Javerbaum, and the rest of the Daily Show staff on *America: The Book (A Citizen's Guide to Democracy Inaction)*. Prior to his work with Comedy Central, he was an editor of *The Onion* in Madison, Wisconsin. He currently lives in New York City, the birthplace of the five-dollar cappuccino.

Rattawut Lapcharoensap is the author of *Sightseeing,* a collection of short stories, which was a finalist for the Guardian First Book Award and the New York Public Library Young Lions Fiction Award. His stories have appeared in *Granta, Zoetrope: All-Story, One Story, Glimmer Train, Best New American Voices,* and *Best American Non-Required Reading.* He lives in New York City.

Beverly Lowry was born in Memphis and reared in Greenville, Mississippi. She is the author of six novels—including *Come Back, Lolly Ray; Daddy's Girl;* and *The Track of Real Desires*—and three books of nonfiction: *Crossed Over: A Murder, A Memoir; Her Dream of Dreams: The Rise and Triumph of Madam C. J. Walker;* and *Harriet Tubman: Imagining a Life.* Her book reviews have appeared in the *New York Times,* the *Houston Chronicle,* and the *Los Angeles Times,* and her essays and feature journalism in various anthologies as well as *The New Yorker, Granta, Rolling Stone, Vanity Fair, Redbook,* and *Ladies' Home Journal.* The past recipient of Guggenheim and Rockefeller fellowships, she teaches in the MFA program at George Mason University. She lives with Tom Johnson in Austin, near her son and not far from Wimberley, where her mother and father lived and are buried.

Haruki Murakami was born in Kyoto in 1949 and now lives near Tokyo. He is the author of the novels *Kafka on the Shore; Sputnik Sweetheart; South of the Border, West of the Sun; The Wind-Up Bird Chronicle; Dance Dance Dance; Hard-Boiled Wonderland and the End of the World; Norwegian Wood;* and *A Wild Sheep Chase,* and of a collection of stories, *The Elephant Vanishes.* He is also the author of the nonfiction work *Underground: The Tokyo Gas At-*

tack and the Japanese Psyche. His work has been translated into sixteen languages.

Phoebe Nobles recommends: Cream-Nut peanut butter from Grand Rapids, Michigan; Riga Gold smoked sprats with Bridgeport India Pale Ale from Portland, Oregon; Rogue River blue cheese; a pulled-pork sandwich at House Park BBQ in Austin; Wilkin and Sons tawny orange marmalade on buttered toast with black tea; Philippe's French dip sandwich in Los Angeles; *banh-mi* from a strip mall in Houston; South Carolina peaches and fireworks at the Georgia border; Edmund Fitzgerald porter from Cleveland; blood sausage and an egg deep-fried in olive oil.

Ann Patchett is the author of five novels, *The Patron Saint of Liars, Taft, The Magician's Assistant, Bel Canto,* and *Run* (forthcoming), as well as a memoir, *Truth & Beauty: A Friendship.* She has been the recipient of a Guggenheim fellowship, the PEN/ Faulkner Award, and England's Orange Prize. She lives in Tennessee.

Anneli Rufus lives in California and is the author of four books, including *The Farewell Chronicles* and *Party of One.* She is the coauthor of five more, including *Weird Europe* and *California Babylon.* Several world-famous restaurants thrive in her town, and she has never set foot inside any of them.

Paula Wolfert is an internationally known cookbook author specializing in Mediterranean cuisine. Her award-winning books include *The Cooking of Southwest France, The Slow Mediterranean*

Kitchen, and *Couscous and Other Good Food from Morocco.* She has won the Julia Child Award (twice), the James Beard Award (three times), the Tastemaker Award, the M. F. K. Fisher Prize, the Cooks Magazine Platinum Plate Award, and the Périgueux Award for Lifetime Achievement. Born in Brooklyn, the mother of two grown children, Paula has lived in Paris, Tangier, Manhattan, northwest Connecticut, and northern California. Married to crime fiction writer William Bayer, she currently lives in the Sonoma Valley.

Permissions Acknowledgments

Acknowledgments

Many thanks to:

The writers whose stories you find here, for their hard work and for contributing their distinctive voices to the project.

Jennifer Joel at ICM, for making it all happen quickly and elegantly, for being reassuring, tough, wise, insightful, and of course for selling the book to the perfect editor.

Megan Lynch at Riverhead, for her enthusiasm, intelligence, imagination, friendship, and for making all aspects of the process fun.

Also at Riverhead: Lisa Amoroso, Susan Baldaserini, Sarah Bowlin, Matt Boyd, Lisa D'Agostino, JoAnna Kremer, Marie Finamore, Doug Jones, Geoff Kloske, Nellys Li, Laurin Lucaire, Catharine Lynch, Alaina Mauro, Katie McKee, Chris Nelson, Meredith Phebus, Marysarah Quinn, Ashley Regan, Melissa Solis, Bonnie Soodek, and Claire Vaccaro.

The University of Michigan, for providing the perfect combination of time, money, and loneliness.

Katie Sigelman, Julie Grau, Anne Stameshkin, Thisbe Nissen, Kathy Belden, Caroline Fidanza, Ken Wiss, Dolsy Smith, Nancy Ferrari, Joe Adler, Susan and Robert Lescher, and all the agents and publishers who lent their support to this project.

The Lapidus and Lerner families, especially Iris, for being completely engaged in the project from beginning to end, Adam, for phrasing everything so memorably, and Steven.

My family of friends, particularly Penny Boyle, Amelia Corona, and Rachel Dannefer, with whom I learned how to cook.

Jofie, for his ability to recognize a good idea, taking me to the library, listening to me talk about this book for two years (and counting), remaining enthusiastic, providing every sort of help, encouragement, and support, and laughing every time I said to him, "You're really going in the acknowledgments now."